1st Workshop on EVENTS: Definition, Detection, Coreference, and Representation 2013

Atlanta, Georgia, USA
14 June 2013

ISBN: 978-1-62993-004-6

Printed from e-media with permission by:

Curran Associates, Inc.
57 Morehouse Lane
Red Hook, NY 12571

Some format issues inherent in the e-media version may also appear in this print version.

Printed by Curran Associates, Inc. (2013)

For permission requests, please contact the Association for Computational Linguistics at the address below.

Association for Computational Linguistics
209 N. Eighth Street
Stroudsburg, Pennsylvania 18360

Phone: 1-570-476-8006
Fax: 1-570-476-0860

acl@aclweb.org

Additional copies of this publication are available from:

Curran Associates, Inc.
57 Morehouse Lane
Red Hook, NY 12571 USA
Phone: 845-758-0400
Fax: 845-758-2634
Email: curran@proceedings.com
Web: www.proceedings.com

NAACL HLT 2013

The 1st Workshop on EVENTS: Definition, Detection, Coreference, and Representation

Proceedings of the Conference

14 June 2013
Westin Peachtree Plaza Hotel
Atlanta, Georgia

Introduction

The definition and detection of events has its roots in philosophy and linguistics, with seminal works by Davidson (1969; 1985), Quine (1985), and Parsons (1990). Though events have long been a subject of study, the NLP community has yet to achieve a consensus on the treatment of events, in spite of its critical importance to several areas in natural language processing, such as topic detection and tracking (Allan et al., 1998), information extraction (Humphreys et al., 1997), question answering (Narayanan and Harabagiu, 2004), textual entailment (Haghighi et al., 2005), and contradiction detection (De Marneffe et al., 2008). Most attempts to provide annotation of event coreference have been limited to specific scenarios or domains, as in LDC's ACE and Machine Reading event annotation (Humphreys et al., 1997; Bagga and Baldwin, 1999; He, 2007). The recent OnotoNotes annotations include more general event mentions and coreference, but mainly identify coreferences between verbs and nominalizations (Pradhan, 2007). Events are also a central element of the Time-ML temporal relation annotation, with an overlap-ping but slightly different approach (Pustejovsky, et al., 2010).

Truly comprehensive event detection must encompass the detection of events and their subevents, and take into account bridging references (Poesio and Artstein, 2005; 2008). The requisite event representation is clearly related to the information available in lexical resources such as PropBank, VerbNet, and FrameNet, but goes well beyond anything they currently contain. Bejan and Harabagiu (2010) have recently offered broader event coreference annotation for evaluation purposes, which was revised and extended by Lee et al., (2012). The organizers are themselves involved in event coreference projects for deep natural language understanding and medical informatics.

The time is ripe to bring together people interested in a serious discussion about the nature, definition, recognition, and representation of events and their parts and aspects. As a community we have to develop appropriate guidelines, resources, and processes for dealing with events and inter-event coreference.

In this workshop we structure the discussion around three themes:

- Foundations: What are Events? Definition and recognition.
- Coreference: When are two events the same? What kinds of identity are there?
- Representation: How best to represent events and event groups?

This is a genuine "working" workshop. Leading up the workshop, the organizers, with the assistance of the program committee, organized a shared annotation task on event mention and coreference annotation. Data was made available for participants to annotate, and the resulting annotations were analyzed for agreements and disagreements. During the workshop, the principal differences emerging from the different annotation schemes will be highlighted and discussed, with the intention of reaching a consensus on the handling of events and their coreference in future work in the NLP community. We have invited James Pustejovsky, the leader of the Time-ML effort, whose contribution as the keynote address are much appreciated.

We hope that this workshop will be the beginning of a concerted effort to come to grips with the challenging topic of events.

Reference

1. James Allan, Jaime Carbonell, George Doddington, Jonathan Yamron, and Yiming Yang. 1998. Topic Detection and Tracking Pilot Study: Final Report. *Proceedings of the Broadcast News Understanding and Transcription Workshop*, pp 194–218.

2. Amit Bagga and Breck Baldwin. 1998. Algorithms for scoring coreference chains. *Proceedings of the LREC 1998 Workshop on Linguistic Coreference*, pp 563–566.

3. Amit Bagga and Breck Baldwin. 1999. Cross-document event coreference: Annotations, experiments, and observations. *Proceedings of the ACL 1999 Work-shop on Coreference and its Applications*, pp 1–8.

4. Cosmin Adrian Bejan and Sanda Harabagiu. 2010. Unsupervised Event Coreference Resolution with Rich Linguistic Features. *Proceedings of the 48th Annual Meeting of the Association for Computational Linguistics (ACL)*, Uppsala, Sweden.

5. Zheng Chen and Heng Ji. 2009. Graph-based event co-reference resolution. *Proceedings of the ACL-IJCNLP 2009 Workshop on Graph-based Methods for Natural Language Processing*, pp 54–57.

6. Donald Davidson, 1969. The Individuation of Events. In N. Rescher et al., eds., *Essays in Honor of Carl G. Hempel*, Dordrecht: Reidel. Reprinted in D. Davidson, ed., *Essays on Actions and Events*, 2001, Oxford: Clarendon Press.

7. Donald Davidson, 1985. Reply to Quine on Events, pp 172–176. In E. LePore and B. McLaughlin, eds., *Actions and Events: Perspectives on the Philosophy of Donald Davidson*, Oxford: Blackwell.

8. Marie-Catherine de Marneffe, Anna N. Rafferty, and Christopher D. Manning. 2008. Finding Contradictions in Text. *Proceedings of the 46th Annual Meeting of the Association for Computational Linguistics: Human Language Technologies (ACL-HLT)*, pp 1039–1047.

9. Aria Haghighi, Andrew Ng, and Christopher Manning. 2005. Robust Textual Inference via Graph Matching. *Proceedings of Human Language Technology Conference and Conference on Empirical Methods in Natural Language Processing (HLT-EMNLP)*, pp 387–394.

10. Tian He. 2007. *Coreference Resolution on Entities and Events for Hospital Discharge Summaries*. Thesis, Massachusetts Institute of Technology.

11. Kevin Humphreys, Robert Gaizauskas, and Saliha Azzam. 1997. Event coreference for information extraction. *Proceedings of the Workshop On Operational Factors In Practical Robust Anaphora Resolution For Unrestricted Texts*, pp 75–81.

12. Srini Narayanan and Sanda Harabagiu. 2004. Question Answering Based on Semantic Structures. *Proceedings of the 20th International Conference on Computational Linguistics (COLING)*, pp 693–701.

13. Massimo Poesio and Ron Artstein. 2005. Annotating (anaphoric) ambiguity. *Corpus Linguistics*, Birmingham, UK.

14. Massimo Poesio and Ron Artstein. 2008. Anaphoric annotation in the ARRAU corpus. *Proceedings of the LREC 2008 conference*, Marrakech, Morocco.

15. Sameer Pradhan, Eduard Hovy, Mitch Marcus, Martha Palmer, Lance Ramshaw and Ralph Weischedel, 2007. OntoNotes: A Unified Relational Semantic Representation, *Proceedings of the First IEEE International Conference on Semantic Computing*, Irvine, CA. Best Paper Award.

16. James Pustejovsky, Kiyong Lee, Harry Bunt, and Laurent Romary. 2010. ISO-TimeML: An International Standard for Semantic Annotation. *Proceedings of the LREC 2010 conference*. Malta.

17. William V. O. Quine, 1985. Events and Reification, pp 162–171. In E. LePore and B. P. McLaughlin, eds.,*Actions and Events: Perspectives on the philosophy of Donald Davidson*, Oxford: Blackwell. Reprinted

Organizers:

Eduard Hovy, CMU
Teruko Mitamura, CMU
Martha Palmer, University of Colorado Boulder

Program Committee:

Marjorie Freeman, BBN
Alan Goldschen, Mitre
Kira Griffit, LDC
Heng Ji, CUNY
Boyan Onyshkevych, DOD
Stephanie Strassel, LDC
Ben Van Durme, JHU-COE
Mihai Surdeanu, University of Arizona
Marta Recasens, then at Stanford University

Invited Speaker:

James Pustejovsky, Brandeis University

Table of Contents

Conference Program

Friday, June 14, 2013

9:00–9:15 Welcome

9:15–9:30 Working Session Instructions

9:30–10:30 Invited Talk: The Role of Event-based Representations and Reasoning in Language, James Pustejovsky

10:30–11:00 Break

11:00–12:00 Working Session I: What are events?

12:00–1:00 Poster Session

Coping With Implicit Arguments And Events Coreference
Rodolfo Delmonte

GAF: A Grounded Annotation Framework for Events
Antske Fokkens, Marieke van Erp, Piek Vossen, Sara Tonelli, Willem Robert van Hage, Luciano Serafini, Rachele Sprugnoli and Jesper Hoeksema

Events are Not Simple: Identity, Non-Identity, and Quasi-Identity
Eduard Hovy, Teruko Mitamura, Felisa Verdejo, Jun Araki and Andrew Philpot

Event representation across genre
Lidia Pivovarova, Silja Huttunen and Roman Yangarber

A Semantic Tool for Historical Events
Ryan Shaw

Annotating Change of State for Clinical Events
Lucy Vanderwende, Fei Xia and Meliha Yetisgen-Yildiz

2:00–3:30 Working Session II: When are two events the same? What relations are between events?

3:30–4:00 Break

Friday, June 14, 2013 (continued)

4:00–5:30	Working Session III: How best to represent events? What aspects to annotate?
5:30–6:00	General Discussion
6:00	Close

Coping With Implicit Arguments And Events Coreference

Rodolfo Delmonte
Department of Language Studies & Department of Computer Science
Ca' Foscari University - 30123, Venezia, Italy
delmont@unive.it

Abstract

In this paper we present ongoing work for the creation of a linguistically-based system for event coreference. We assume that this task requires deep understanding of text and that statistically-based methods, both supervised and unsupervised are inadequate. The reason for this choice is due to the fact that event coreference can only take place whenever argumenthood is properly computed. It is a fact that in many cases, arguments of predicates are implicit and thus linguistically unexpressed. This prevents training to produce sensible results. We also assume that spatiotemporal locations need to be taken into account and this is also very often left implicit. We used GETARUNS system to develop the coreference system which works on the basis of the discourse model and the automatically annotated markables. We present data from the analysis, both on unexpressed implicit arguments and the description of the coreference algorithm.

1 Introduction

NLP processing is more and more oriented towards semantic processing which in turn requires deep understanding of texts. We assume that this is only possible if unexpressed implicit linguistic elements and semantically deficient items are taken into consideration (Delmonte 2009a, 2009b). One of the first problem in the analysis of any text is accounting for implicit or linguistically unexpressed information. This kind of information is not available in dependecy-based current annotated corpora or is only partially available – as in Penn Treebank – but it cannot possibly be learnt. The problem of null and pronominal elements is paramount in the recovery of Predicate-Argument Structures which constitutes the fundamental element onto which propositional semantics is made to work. However, applying machine learning techniques on available treebanks is of no help. State of the art systems are using more and more dependency representations which have lately shown great resiliency, robustness, scalability and great adaptability for semantic enrichment and processing. However, by far the majority of systems available off the shelf don't support a fully semantically consistent representation and lack Null Elements or Antecedents for pronominal ones.

If we limit ourselves to Null Elements, and to PennTreebank (hence PT), we may note that Marcus ('94) referred explicitly to Predicate-Argument Structures (hence PASs) and to the need to address this level of annotation. He mentions explicitly that "we intend to automatically extract a bank of PASs intended at the very least for parser evaluation from the resulting annotated corpus" and further on "the notation should make it easy to automatically recover PAS" (ibid. 121). He also mentions the need to allow for a clear and concise distinction between verb ARGUMENTs and ADJUNCTs, which he asserts to be very difficult to make, consistently. This happens to be true: the final version of PT II does not include coindexing in controversial cases and has coindexing for null SBJ only in a percentage of the cases. PT contains 36862 cases of null elements (including traces, expletives, gapping and ambiguity) as listed in Johansson(2007), over 93532 simple clauses and 55600 utterances, for a percentage of 66.3%. Of course this number does not include pronominal arguments which need to be bound – and are not bound in PT - to an antecedent in order to become semantically consistent.

As to PT, the difficulty of the task is testified by the presence of non coindexed Null Elements: in particular we see that they are 8416, that is 22.83%. If we exclude all traces of WH and topicalization and limit ourselves to the category OTHER TRACES which includes all unexpressed SUBJects of infinitivals and gerundives, we come up with 12172 cases of Null non-coindexed elements, 33% of all cases. We should note that for how much large this number may seem, this still represents a small percentage when compared to the number of null elements in languages like Chinese or Romance languages like Italian, which allow for free null subjects insertion in tensed clauses.

Current statistically dependency parsers have made improvements in enriching their structural output representation (Gabbard et al. 2006; Sagae and Tsujii, 2008; Choi & Palmer, 2010; Cai et al. 2011). However, coindexation is not always performed: when it is, its performance is computed separately because it is lower than accuracy for labeled/unlabeled tasks. In particular, Schmid reports 84% F-score for empty elements prediction and 77% for coindexation on PT. However, other parsers have much worse results, with Johnson(2001) being the worst, with 68% F-score. The presence of additional difficulties to predict empty categories is the cause of a bad drop in performance in Chinese - no more than 50% accuracy reported by Cai et al. (2011) compared to 74/77% of the labeled/unlabeled task. Results reported by Yang & Xue (2010) on recovering labeled empty elements in an experiment carried on a small subset of the Penn Chinese Treebank 6.0 reach an average of 60.5% of F-measure. As to recovery of specific items, we note that over a total number of 290 little_pro items recall fares around 50%.

Of course the phenomenon is very much language dependent, as discussed above. If we consider a language like Italian – which we described fully from structures annotated in the treebank called VIT (Delmonte 2004) – we can see that in addition to untensed sentences also simple clauses with tensed verbs show the same problem. In fact, over 66.5% (9634 over 15874) of all simple clauses are subjectless, they have an omitted or unexpressed subject which is marked in linguistics with a little_pro and the agreement coming from morphology of the main verb. Of the remaining lexically expressed subjects, only 64% (6166 over 9634) are in canonical position, that is in preverbal position and adjacent to the inflected verb. The remaining 36% of lexically expresses subjects are positioned to the right or are separated from the verb by other constituents.

2 Events and Null Elements

We will now try to describe events in terms of the contribution of Null Elements. Events are mainly characterized by their meaning which is defined in a gloss or by one or more semantic categories, or even by a synset of synonym concepts. In addition to that, events may be regarded as being composed of two other elements:

- the participants to the event, which are arguments and adjuncts or circumstantials

- the spatiotemporal location of the event

Both components may be linguistically expressed or be left implicit and thus should be inferred from previous discourse. In fact the spatiotemporal location of the event is usually indicated explicitly only if needed and is mostly left unexpressed. Participants on the contrary are mostly explicitly expressed before they can be left implicit. However, in some case, participants are linguistically unexpressed for structural reasons or else expressed by a pronoun. Both cases require a deep system or a deep parser together with a pronominal binding algorithm to be in place, in order to find the appropriate antecedent and bind the empty arguments. There are exceptions to these rules and they are constituted by utterances of generic or arbitrary reference, something intended in utterances such as,

(1) Doing regular physical exercise is strongly recommended at a certain age.

where no participant is explicitly indicated, but it is clearly understood by inferences determined by knowledge of the world.

Events may be coreferred or may be queried: in both cases, we are also dealing with semantic relations at discourse structure level. The need to corefer to a previous event derives from conversational or argumentative strategies. Generally speaking, it is due to the need of expanding concepts and facts reported in the previous mention. At a discourse level, this is usually called ELABORATION or EXPLANATION. Other possible cases of event coreference at discourse structure level can be due to the need of enriching the previous description of additional facts cooccuring with the previously mentioned event: in this case we may have an hypernymic or an hyponymic relation intervening

between the two facts or concepts. Let's look at some examples taken from the demo text made available by the organizers.
After the title, we have a first event description, reported by a newspaper, which is a violent event followed by an adjunct clause describing the effects or caused consequences: we capitalize event naming words and then indicate the semantic discourse relation:

"A Kurdish newspaper said Wednesday that Iraqi members of an Al Qaeda-linked group, a Kurd and an Arab, ***BLEW*** themselves up in northern Iraq on February 1, ***KILLING*** at least 105 people."

CAUSE ➔ BLOW, KILL

The idea in this case is that the two events are linked by a semantic relation rather than simply the first event being coreferred by the second. The text continues by expanding the event introducing some comment that elaborates on the previous sentence:

"The twin suicide bombing ***WAS*** the deadliest attack in post-war Iraq and ***WAS SUSPECTED TO HAVE BEEN CARRIED OUT*** by foreign fighters, possibly linked to Osama bin Laden's Al-Qaeda network."

ELABORATION ➔ BOMBING, ATTACK

CAUSE ➔ BOMBING, BLOW

EXPLANATION ➔ SUSPECT(CARRY_OUT), BLOW

Discourse relations are triggered by event coreference which in this sentence is achieved by two nominalizations: in fact only definite expressions are taken into consideration, in particular if singular in number. The first one is TWIN SUICIDE BOMBING which we understand to be a new enriched mention of BLOW at first by a causal relation intervening between BOMB and BLOW. This semantic relation is not available from WordNet but from Sumo-Milo, where the verbs BOMB, BLAST, ATTACK, KILL, and FIGHT all share one semantic class, VIOLENT_CONTEST and/or DESTRUCTION with BLOW. The causal relation is derived from commonsense knowledge available in "ConceptNet" by the AI Laboratory of MIT. Searching for relations intervening between BOMB and BLOW_UP, this is what you can find - represented in an appropriate Prolog-like format:

```
cpn(udf,bomb,[blow,something,up]).
cpn(udf,bomb,[blow,things,up]).
cpn(udf,bomb,[blow,up,buildings]).
cpn(udf,bomb,[blow,up,stuff]).
cpn(udf,bomb,blow).
cpn(do,person,[don_t,want,be,blow,up,by,bomb]).
cpn(dof,person,[not,be,blow,up,by,bomb]).
```

They are also all classified as NEGATIVE polarity items and are part of the same Lexical Field in Roget's Thesaurus.
Then the additional contribution of its arguments, where "blowing themselves up" implies a SUICIDE took place. At the same time, the use of "twin" is coreferring with "members" a plural noun, better specified as being composed of two individuals "a Kurd and an Arab" in an apposition to it. Thus, the nominalization does not add any new information that could not be understood from previous mention, but certainly clarifies previous information thus respecting Grice's maxims.
The copulative structure headed by WAS, is used to assign a property to the coreferred event thus contributing new information. We now know that the newspaper reports the event as being "the deadliest attack in post-war Iraq". We also learn that the two fighters identity was suspected to be not Iraqi but possibly "foreign", deemed to belong to bin Laden's network. All of this new information can be labeled as "Explanation".
The news story continues by elaborating on the two fighters by expanding on their identity, and then explaining the way in which the bombing was organized in the following two sentences.

"The pair ***were named*** respectively as Abu Bakr Hawleri and Kazem Al-Juburi, alias Abu Turab, by independent newspaper Hawlani, which ***said*** they ***belonged*** to the Army of Ansar al-Sunna.

The Kurd ***blew*** himself up in the offices of the Patriotic Union of Kurdistan (PUK) and the Arab in the offices of the Kurdistan Democratic Party (KDP), both in the Kurdish city of Arbil, ***said*** the newspaper.

Each one ***carried*** a belt packed with four kilograms (8.8 pounds) of TNT mixed with phosphorus, a highly flammable material, the newspaper ***said***."

The use of a definite singular expression is highly indicative of the coreference mechanism being activated. This applies to THE PAIR, coreferring with "Iraqi members" and also with "twin". The same can be said of "The Kurd" coreferring with the previous mention and also the use of the same predicate BLOW UP. In the following stretch of discourse, the story corefers to the "Army of Ansar al-Sunna", to explain the role that the organization had in the bombing:

"Ansar al-Sunna last week ***claimed*** the twin bombings in a statement ***posted*** on an Islamist website. The newspaper ***said*** the motive of the attack was to "***punish***" the two Kurdish secular groups, which ***control*** Iraqi Kurdistan, for their alliance with the US-led coalition.

The newspaper ***said*** Ansar al-Sunna ***broke away from*** the Ansar al-Islam group last October and was ***led*** by an Arab whose alias ***is*** Abu Abdullah Hasan bin Mahmud. Ansar al-Sunna ***is*** more extreme, ***said*** the newspaper."

The first coreference link is expressed by the sentence "Ansar claimed the TWIN BOMBINGs" which is used to expand on the role of the organization of the original event. Additional events are the STATEMENT, a nominal event, and the MOTIVE OF THE ATTACK which introduces the MOTIVATION for the event. This causal link is connected to actual causal event: PUNISHing the Kurdish group controlling Iraqi Kurdistan. In turn, the action of PUNISHing is explained by another eventive nominalization, the ALLIANCE of the group (the possessive THEIR corefers with it), with the US-led coalition.
Additional explanation is reported in the final sentence (longer than 40 tokens!!) where the relation intervening between the motive the attack as contained in the statement and previously occurring facts is further clarified:

"The newspaper ***added*** that bin Mahmud ***is*** the brother of man whose alias ***is*** Abdullah Al-Shami, an Ansar al-Islam leader who was ***killed*** last year while ***fighting*** a US-backed onslaught by the PUK that ***forced*** the group out of its enclave near the Iranian border at the end of March last year."

The sentence contains additional coreferring nominalizations like ONSLAUGHT, which reminds of the bombing and of the previous attack. The overall events description is rich in temporal and spatial locations which contribute to the understanding and the overall discourse structure. In particular we start out by a spatial location, NORTHERN IRAQ, and a temporal location, FEBRUARY 1st. Both locations remain the same in the following sentences until we reach a change in topics and locations. This happens when "Ansar al-Sunna" is introduced as SUBJect of CLAIM, an event location in time, LAST WEEK. Additional information the Ansar al-Islam group takes us back to LAST OCTOBER. Eventually, in the final sentence, we have been told that the current bombing event may have relation with the killing of another Ansar al-Islam leader, during an ONSLAUGHT that took place LAST YEAR, in a different location, NEAR THE IRANIAN BORDER. The generic location LAST_YEAR is further specified as being END OF MARCH.

3. GETARUNS : a system for text understanding

GETARUNS[1], the system for text understanding developed at the University of Venice, is organized as a pipeline which includes two versions of the system: what we call the Partial and the Deep GETARUNS and they work in a backoff policy. There are in fact three parsers interconnected and they are activated in order to prevent failure to take place. The system has a middle module for semantic interpretation and discourse model construction which is cast into Situation Semantics; and a higher module where reasoning and generation takes place.

The system is based on LFG theoretical

1 The system has been tested in STEP competition (see Delmonte 2008), and can be downloaded in two separate places. The partial system called VENSES in its stand-alone version is available at http://www.aclweb.org/aclwiki/index.php?title=Textual_Entailment_Resource_Pool. The complete deep system is available both at http://www.sigsem.org/wiki/STEP_2008_shared_task:_comparing_semantic_representations, and at, http://project.cgm.unive.it/html/sharedtask/.

framework and has a highly interconnected modular structure.

The output of grammatical modules is fed then onto the Binding Module which activates an algorithm for anaphoric binding. Antecedents for pronouns are ranked according to grammatical function, semantic role, inherent features and their position at f-structure. Eventually, this information is added into the original f-structure graph and then passed on to the Discourse Module (hence DM).

GETARUNS, has a linguistically based semantic module which is used to build up the DM. Semantic processing is strongly modularized and distributed amongst a number of different submodules which take care of Spatio-Temporal Reasoning, Discourse Level Anaphora Resolution, and other subsidiary processes like Topic Hierarchy which cooperate to find the most probable antecedent of coreferring and cospecifying referential expressions when creating semantic individuals. These are then asserted in the DM, which is then the sole knowledge representation used to solve nominal coreference. The system uses two resolution submodules which work in sequence: the first one is fired whenever a free sentence external pronoun is spotted; the second one takes the results of the first submodule and checks for nominal anaphora. They have access to all data structures contemporarily and pass the resolved pair, anaphor-antecedent to the following modules. Semantic Mapping is performed in two steps: at first a Logical Form is produced which is a structural mapping from DAGs onto unscoped well-formed formulas. These are then turned into situational semantics informational units, infons which may become facts or sits. Each unit has a relation, a list of arguments which in our case receive their semantic roles from lower processing – a polarity, a temporal and a spatial location index.

All entities and their properties are asserted in the DM with the relations in which they are involved; in turn the relations may have modifiers - sentence level adjuncts, and entities may also have modifiers and attributes. Each entity has a polarity and a couple of spatiotemporal indices which are linked to main temporal and spatial locations if any exists; else they are linked to presumed time reference derived from tense and aspect computation. On second occurrence of the same nominal head the semantic index is recovered from the history list and the system checks whether it is the same referring expression and has non-conflicting attributes or properties. In all other cases a new entity is asserted in the DM which however is also computed as being included in (a superset of) or by (a subset of) the previous entity.

4. A System For Event Marking And Event Coreference

I will now go through the text above indicating places where the system has been able to locate and identify missing arguments. In order to clarify the working of the system I will use the output of the discourse model, which contains fully coreferred empty or linguistically unexpressed elements which have gone through pronominal binding process as well as coreference analysis.

The first unexpressed element is the subject of the adjunct gerundive headed by KILL in the first sentence:

(1) A Kurdish newspaper said Wednesday that Iraqi members of an Al Qaeda-linked group, a Kurd and an Arab, blew themselves up in northern Iraq on February 1, killing at least 105 people.

The second unexpressed argument is contained in sentence 2, in the infinitival governed by SUSPECT and headed by CARRY_OUT, which is contained in the coordinate structure headed by SUSPECT,

(2) The twin suicide bombing was the deadliest attack in post-war Iraq and was suspected to have been carried out by foreign fighters, possibly linked to Osama bin Laden's Al-Qaeda network.

where the suicide_bombing is predicated as the "deadliest attack" in the previous main sentence. The main spatial location now becomes Iraq. Another unexpressed argument is the subject of POSTED, a participial modifying STATEMENT,

(3) Ansar al-Sunna last week claimed the twin bombings in a statement posted on an Islamist website.

where we still want to know who posted the "statement", and the information is passed by the

main clause as the subject of CLAIM, i.e. Ansar al-Sunna.
Then we have another infinitival lacking subject argument information, in the following sentence,

(4) The newspaper said the motive of the attack was to "punish" the two Kurdish secular groups, which control Iraqi Kurdistan, for their alliance with the US-led coalition.

This is a copulative structure where the subject MOTIVE is predicated by the infinitival headed by PUNISH. In fact, this verb is lacking a referential subject simply because the predication prevents it from having a specific one.
The same GROUP is coreferred in the final sentence that contains the most important sequence of unexpressed but yet essential arguments:

(5) The newspaper added that bin Mahmud is the brother of man whose alias is Abdullah Al-Shami, an Ansar al-Islam leader who was killed last year while fighting a US-backed onslaught by the PUK that forced the group out of its enclave near the Iranian border at the end of March last year.

The gerundive headed by FIGHT has LEADER as SUBJect and as OBJect the GROUP we found in the previous sentence. It is important to notice that this mention of GROUP is NOT coreferent with the one appearing at the beginning of the text. This non coreference is clearly apparent from attributes accompanying the head: the first one is expressed as "an Al Qaeda-linked group", whereas the second as "the two Kurdish secular groups".
In the final computation, the system produces a set of entity pools, that is a set of all referents to a given semantic index - be they properties, entities or relations. In particular, the referent to the LEADER coincides by virtue of a predication, with Abdullah Al-Shami and has the property of being associated to Ansar al-Islam: from the pool, we now know that he was KILLED, being associated to the THEME_AFFected role.

4.1 The Experiment and an Evaluation

We tested the coreference module with the sample text and produced the following output that we comment in this section. For each event we have two vectors of information that we then use to evaluate its relevance and its possible coreference in the previous text. The categories used are fully explained in Delmonte (2007; 2009) and here we limit ourselves to a short description.
The event may be a verb and be related to a propositional analysis or be a noun. Nouns classified as activity or events are selected as markables: this classification is partially derived from NomBank associated information about eventive nominals. Coreference links are activated by synonymity or just similarity, measured by WordNet synset, a Thesaurus or sharing identical semantic classes as indicated in SUMO-MILO or other similar computational lexica. The certainty value varies accordingly: from more certain, say .9, to less certain .4. Obviously, copulative predications are marked with certainty equal to 1 being properties predicated in the syntax of the subject.

4.1.1 Coreference links

We present here briefly the addition to the system GETARUNS that have been produced for this task. The annotation of each text is shown in an xml file which has been obtained in the following steps:
a. the system GETARUNS produces a deep analysis of each text on a sentence by sentence basis. At the end of the analysis of each sentence, markables are collected and all semantic information is attached to each word of the sentence. We collected all verbs and also eventive nominals and possible eventive modifiers. This is done in two steps.
b. at the end of parsing each word of the sentence is associated to its lemma and general semantic categories are also collected from the analysis.
c. The system produces then the steps required for the Discourse Model which is where entities, relations and properties are asserted with their attributes. Semantic indices are assigned to each new entity and previous mentions receive previously assigned indices. At this point the contents of the discourse model are associated to each word of the sentence.
d. At the end of the analysis of the text the system collects all markables, which are internally made of four elements: an markable index, a word, a lemma, a semantic index (from the discourse model) or a generic indicator of eventuality for all verbs.

e. Then the complete discourse model is searched to produce a list of all entities, relations and properties with their spatiotemporal relations and polarity, as documented in situation semantics. Additional information is derived in this phase from WordNet, FrameNet or SumoMilo ontology and is made available to the coreference algorithm. Another component that is activated at the end of the analysis is sentiment analysis that computes an affective label associated to each markable - if possible - and classifies each markable into three different classes: positive, negative and neutral.

d. The coreference algorithm works as follows: for each markable it check all possible coreference links, at first on the basis only of inherent semantic features, which are: wordform and lemma identity; then semantic similarity measured on the basis of a number of similarity criteria which are lexically based (no statistical measure is used). We search WordNet synsets and assign a score according to whether the markables are directly contained in the same synset or not. A different score is assigned if their relation can be inferred from the hierarchy. Other computational lexical resources we use are those documented in our work on Text Entailment Recognition (Delmonte et al. 2005; 2006; 2007; 2008), and include FrameNet and Frames hierarchy; SumoMilo and its semantic classification.

f. After collecting all possible coreferential relations between semantically validated markables, we then proceed to filter out those links that are inconsistent or incompatible according to three criteria:

- first criterion: diverse sentiment polarity
- second criterion: different argument structure
- third criterion: non related spatiotemporal relations

Both argument structure and spatiotemporal relations are collected in the discourse structure which also contains dependence relations expressed by discourse relations in discourse structures; temporal logical relations as computed from an adaptation of Allen's algorithm; and a point of view computed on the basis of presence of "reportive" verbs, or direct speech, reported speech, reported indirect speech.

Another criterion we adopt is the nature of semantic similarity computed by the system. Values below a certain threshold indicate the coreference has been chosen on the basis of weak similarity, as may apply to semantic lexical fields. These are based on thesauri classification. Some examples below.

As said above, event coreference links require sentiment match, argument identity or semantic similarity. In particular consider such cases as

<MARK ID=m34> claimed </MARK>.

is semantically computed as a communication verb on a par with SAY, but coreference is prevented by the fact that arguments don't coincide. SAY in all its various forms is used to report what the newspaper Hawlani said. Here CLAIM is related to different arguments as shown in the discourse structure entry,

ds(to(7-17),7-18,claim([id86:[ansar,sunna,al],id4:suspect,id87:statement],1,id71),during(tes(sn19evs7),tes(sn31evs6)), narration,'ansar_al-sunna')

The same applies to the use of KILL in the last sentence (11) whose argument structure prevents a coreference link with the previous occurrence of an identical verb form in sentence (2). Here below are the two discourse structures containing argument structures for the verb KILL in the two sentences:

ds(down(11-28),11-29,kill([id140:[[abdullah,shami,al],leader],id145:exist],1,id71), after(tes(f562evs11),tes(f772evs11)), narration,narrator),

ds(to(2-3),2-4,kill([id16:member,id18:people],1,univ),after(tes(f4_evs_2),tes(f2_evs_1)),result,narrator),

Discourse Structures also contain temporal logical relations, Discourse relation and Point of View. If we consider all computed markables, which are in our system 67, we come up with 47 possible coreference links. However only 17 have been regarded admissible and consistent and are listed here below.

1.coref-ident m1 m7 hypothetical_certainty 1
2.coref-ident m3 m17 hypothetical_certainty 1
3.coref-simil m2 m20 hypothetical_certainty 0.9
4.coref-simil m4 m14 hypothetical_certainty 0.9
5.coref-ident m7 m25 hypothetical_certainty 1
6.coref-simil m10 m21 hypothetical_certainty 0.9
7.coref-ident m6 m28 hypothetical_certainty 1

8.coref-ident m7 m29 hypothetical_certainty 1
9.coref-ident m7 m33 hypothetical_certainty 1
10.coref-simil m1 m36 hypothetical_certainty 0.9
11.coref-simil m11 m35 hypothetical_certainty 0.9
12.coref-simil m15 m37 hypothetical_certainty 0.9
13.coref-ident m6 m43 hypothetical_certainty 1
14.coref-ident m7 m38 hypothetical_certainty 1
15.coref-ident m14 m40 hypothetical_certainty 1
16.coref-simil m32 m47 hypothetical_certainty 0.9
17.coref-ident m7 m48 hypothetical_certainty 1

Markables M1, M7, M25, M33, M38, M48 all refer to verb SAY and have as SUBJect the newspaper; in one case M1 is wrongly coreferred to M36, STATEMENT. M3 is attached to the noun SUSPECT and is made to corefer to M17, the verb SUSPECT which share arguments with the noun. M2 is "Al_Qaeda-linked" and is coreferred to M20, "linked". M4 is BLASTS and is coreferred to M14, ATTACK. M10 is TWIN and is coreferred to M21, PAIR. M6 is "Kurdish" coreferred to M28 again Kurdish, but also M43. M11 is "suicide_bombing" which corefers to M35, "bombings". M15 is "post-war" and is wrongly coreferred to M37 "posted". M14 ATTACK is coreferred to M40 again ATTACK. M32 MIXED is wrongly coreferred to M47 COALITION. There are three errors over 17. Omitted links include the following one
coref- (m4- (blasts-blast-id5))- (m8- (blew-blow_up-id26))-5
where coreference between BLAST and BLOW_UP is established and the score assigned is 0.5. This score is regarded too low and is filtered out, even though a causal link was clearly inferrable.

5. Conclusion and Future Work

We show here below in Table 1. total counts for the 13 texts distributed with the Event Coreference Task. The system computed automatically Controllers and Antecedents: the first are referred to syntactically controlled Null Elements of Relative and Interrogative Clauses. The second are referred to SUBJects of infinitivals, and other predicative structures both argumental and non-argumental. The table also includes counts of Markables and Coreferent Links, again computed automatically. There is no evaluation yet available. What we wanted to show is the proportion of NEs with respect to sentences, which is 1.6 per sentence, that is there are three NEs every two sentences.

LI/Rounds	Round1	Round2	Round3	**Total**
Markables	334	372	325	1031
Corefs	72	79	37	188
Controllers	69	57	55	181
Antecedents	60	57	53	170
Sentences	69	78	72	219
Total Null Elementss	129	114	108	351

Table 1. Null Elements, Markables and Coreferents automatically computed by Getaruns on the 13 texts of the Task

In this paper we presented ongoing work to produce a system for event coreference that uses a linguistically-based approach and the output of a deep system for the representation of a text in a situation semantics framework. The output of the system on the sample text has been fairly consistent in particular for what concerns the computation of implicit information which we regard paramount for a successful performance in the task at hand.
Semantic relations have been built taking into due account all attributes and modifiers of the semantic head. This process has allowed preventing coreference to take place on the basis of simple concept matching procedures. Some inferential processes have been fired using commonsense knowledge stored in the publicly available resource, ConceptNet.
Besides, the computation of temporal relations based on a revised version of Allen's algorithm has allowed to control inclusion relations intervening between event structures. The output of the system includes a discourse structure which shows coordination and subordination links between discourse stretches defined by propositional level analysis. Structural inclusion is allowed again only in presence of same TOPIC and same spatiotemporal relation checking. Both NEW topic and NEW spatiotemporal relation will cause the structure to jump up to any possible previous node that may be used to provide a cohesion link in the text. This notion of coreference has not been explored yet and will be the topic of further study.

REFERENCES

Alshawi, H., Pi-Chuan Chang, M. Ringgaard. (2011). Deterministic Statistical Mapping of Sentences to Underspecified Semantics, in Johan Bos and Stephen Pulman (editors), Proceedings of the 9th International Conference on Computational Semantics, IWCS,15-24.

Bender, E.M. and D.Flickinger (2005). Rapid prototyping of scalable grammars: Towards modularity in extensions to a language-independent core. in Proc. 2nd IJCNLP-05, Jeju Island, Korea.

Bender, E.M., D.Flickinger, and S.Oepen (2002). The Grammar Matrix: An open-source starter-kit for the rapid development of cross-linguistically consistent broad-coverage precision grammars. In J.Carroll et al.(Eds.), Proc. Workshop Grammar Engineering and Evaluation at COLING19, Taipei, Taiwan, 8-14.

Bresnan, J., 2000. *Lexical-Functional Syntax*, Blackwell.

Cai, Shu, David Chiang, Yoav Goldberg, 2011. Language-Independent Parsing with Empty Elements, in Proceedings of the 49th Annual Meeting of the ACL, 212–216.

Choi, Jinho D., Martha Palmer, 2010. Robust Constituent-to-Dependency Conversion for English, in Proceedings of the 9th International Workshop on Treebanks and Linguistic Theories (TLT'9), 55-66, Tartu, Estonia.

Clark P., C. Fellbaum, J. Hobbs, P. Harrison, W.R.Murray, J. Thompson, 2008. Augmenting WordNet for Deep Understanding of Text, in J.Bos & R.Delmonte(eds.), 2008. ACL-SigSem, STEP (Semantics in Text Processing), College Publications, London, p.45-58.

Copestake, Ann. 2004/2006. Robust Minimal Recursion Semantics, Unpublished draft (downloadable from http://www.cl.cam.ac.uk/~aac10/papers.html).

Copestake, Ann, (2009). Invited Talk: Slacker Semantics: Why Superficiality, Dependency and Avoidance of Commitment can be the Right Way to Go. In: Proceedings of the 12th Conference of the European Chapter of the ACL (EACL 2009), pages 1-9. Athens, Greece, 2009.

Copestake, A., D.Flickinger, C.Pollard, and I.Sag (2005). Minimal recursion semantics: An introduction. Research on Language and Computations 3(4), 281-332.

CoreLex:- http://www.cs.brandeis.edu/~paulb/CoreLex/corelex.html

EuroWordNet:- http://www.illc.uva.nl/EuroWordNet/

Delmonte R.(1990), Semantic Parsing with an LFG-based Lexicon and Conceptual Representations, Computers & the Humanities, 5-6, pp.461-488.

Delmonte R., D.Bianchi(1991), Binding Pronominals with an LFG Parser, Proceeding of the Second International Workshop on Parsing Technologies, Cancun(Messico), ACL 1991, pp.59-72.

Delmonte R.(1995), Lexical Representations: Syntax-Semantics interface and World Knowledge, in Rivista dell'AI*IA (Associazione Italiana di Intelligenza Artificiale), Roma, pp.11-16.

Delmonte R.(1996), Lexical Representations, Event Structure and Quantification, Quaderni Patavini di Linguistica 15, 39-93.

Bianchi D., Delmonte R. (1996), Temporal Logic in Sentence and Discourse, in Atti SIMAI'96, pp.226-228.

Dario Bianchi, Rodolfo Delmonte(1999), Reasoning with A Discourse Model and Conceptual Representations, Proc. VEXTAL, Unipress, pp. 401-411.

Delmonte R.(2002), From Deep to Shallow Anaphora Resolution:, in Proc. DAARC2002 , 4th Discourse Anaphora and Anaphora Resolution Colloquium, Lisbona, pp.57-62.

Delmonte R.(2002), GETARUN PARSER - A parser equipped with Quantifier Raising and Anaphoric Binding based on LFG, Proc. LFG2002 Conference, Athens, pp.130-153, at http://cslipublications.stanford.edu/hand/miscpubsonline.html.

Delmonte R., Sara Tonelli, Marco Aldo Piccolino Boniforti, Antonella Bristot, Emanuele Pianta (2005), VENSES – a Linguistically-Based System for Semantic Evaluation, in Joaquin Quiñonero-Candela, Ido Dagan, Bernardo Magnini, Florence d'Alché-Buc, 2005, Machine Learning Challenges. Evaluating Predictive Uncertainty, Visual Object Classification, and Recognising Textual Entailment.: First PASCAL Machine Learning Challenges Workshop, MLCW 2005, Southampton, UK, April 11-13, 2005, Revised Selected Papers, 344-371.

Delmonte, R., Antonella Bristot, Marco Aldo Piccolino Boniforti and Sara Tonelli, 2006. Another Evaluation of Anaphora Resolution Algorithms and a Comparison with GETARUNS' Knowledge Rich Approach, ROMAND 2006, 11th EACL, Trento, Association for Computational Linguistics, 3-10.

Delmonte, R., A. Bristot, M.A.Piccolino Boniforti and S. Tonelli, 2006. Coping with semantic uncertainty with VENSES, in Bernardo Magnini, Ido Dagan(eds.), Proceedings of the Challenges Workshop - The 2nd PASCAL Recognizing Textual Entailment Challenge, 86-91, Università Ca' Foscari, Venezia.

Delmonte R., (2007), Computational Linguistic Text Processing – Logical Form, Semantic Interpretation, Discourse Relations and Question Answering, Nova Science Publishers, New York.

Delmonte R., A. Bristot, M.A.Piccolino Boniforti, S.Tonelli (2007), Entailment and Anaphora Resolution in RTE3, in Proc. ACL Workshop on Text Entailment and Paraphrasing, Prague, ACL

Madison, USA, pp. 48-53.

Bos Johan & Rodolfo Delmonte (eds.), 2008. Semantics in Text Processing (STEP), Research in Computational Semantics, Vol.1, College Publications, London.

Delmonte R., 2009. Computational Linguistic Text Processing – Lexicon, Grammar, Parsing and Anaphora Resolution, Nova Science Publishers, New York.

Delmonte R., G. Nicolae, S. Harabagiu, C.Nicolae (2007), A Linguistically-based Approach to Discourse Relations Recognition, in B.Sharp & M.Zock(eds.), Natural Language Processing and Cognitive Science, Proc. 4th NLPCS, Funchal, Portugal, INSTICC PRESS, pp. 81-91.

Delmonte R., G. Nicolae, S. Harabagiu (2007), A Linguistically-based Approach to Detect Causality Relations in Unrestricted Text, in Proc. MICAI-2007, IEEE Publications, 173-185.

Delmonte R., 2008. Semantic and Pragmatic Computing with GETARUNS, in Bos & Delmonte (eds.), Semantics in Text Processing (STEP), Research in Computational Semantics, Vol.1, College Publications, London, pp. 287-298.

Delmonte R., E. Pianta, (2009), Computing Implicit Entities and Events for Story Understanding, in H.Bunt, V.Petukhova and S.Wubben(eds.), Proc. Eighth International Conference on Computational Semantics IWCS-8, Tilburg University Press, pp. 277-281.

Delmonte R., (2009), A computational approach to implicit entities and events in text and discourse, in International Journal of Speech Technology (IJST), Springer, pp. 1-14.

Gabbard, Ryan, Mitchell Marcus, Seth Kulick, 2006. Fully Parsing the Penn Treebank, in Proceedings of the HLT Conference of the North American Chapter of the ACL, 184–191.

Grice, H. P., 1975. Logic and Conversation. in P. Cole & J. L. Morgan, Syntax and Semantics, Vol. 3: Speech Acts. New York : Academic Press, 41-58.

Harabagiu, S.M., Miller, G.A., Moldovan, D.I.: eXtended WordNet - A Morphologically and Semantically Enhanced Resource (2003), http://xwn.hlt.utdallas.edu, 1-8.

Hobbs, J. (2005). Toward a useful notion of causality for lexical semantics. Journal of Semantics 22, 181–209.

Hobbs, J. (2008). Encoding commonsense knowledge. Technical report, USC/ISI. http://www.isi.edu/~hobbs/csk.html.

Johansson, R. and P. Nugues. 2007. Extended Constituent-to-dependency Conversion for English. In Proceedings of NODALIDA 2007, Tartu, Estonia.

Johnson. M., 2001. Joint and conditional estimation of tagging and parsing models. In ACL 2001, pages 322–329.

Liu, H., Singh, P. (2004). ConceptNet: A Practical Commonsense Reasoning Toolkit.

Marcus, M., G. Kim, M. Ann Marcinkiewicz, R. Macintyre, A. Bies, M. Ferguson, K. Katz, B. Schasberger, (1994). The Penn Treebank: Annotating Predicate Argument Structure, In ARPA Human Language Technology Workshop, 114-119.

Sagae, K. and Tsujii, J. 2008. Shift-Reduce Dependency DAG Parsing. Proceedings of the 22nd International Conference on Computational Linguistics (Coling 2008). Manchester, UK.

Yang, Yaqin and Nianwen Xue. 2010. Chasing the ghost: recovering empty categories in the Chinese Treebank. In Proc. COLING.Schubert, L. and C. Hwang (1993). Episodic logic: A situational logic for NLP. In Situation Theory and Its Applications, pp. 303–337.

Schubert, L. and C.Hwang (1993). Episodic logic: A situational logic for NLP. In Peter Aczel, David Israel, Yasuhiro Katagiri, and Stanley Peters, (Eds.), Situation Theory and its Applications, vol.3, 303-337.

Tonelli, S. & R. Delmonte, 2011. "Desperately seeking Implicit arguments in text", in RELMS'2011, Workshop on Relational Models of Semantics at ACL 2011 Portland, USA. pp.54-62.

At:http://web.media.mit.edu/~push/ConceptNet.pdf.

GAF: A Grounded Annotation Framework for Events

Antske Fokkens, Marieke van Erp, Piek Vossen
The Network Institute
VU University Amsterdam
antske.fokkens@vu.nl
marieke.van.erp@vu.nl
piek.vossen@vu.nl

Sara Tonelli
FBK
Trento, Italy
satonelli@fbk.eu

Willem Robert van Hage
SynerScope B.V.
Eindhoven, The Netherlands
willem.van.hage@synerscope.com

Luciano Serafini, Rachele Sprugnoli
FBK
Trento, Italy
serafini@fbk.eu
sprugnoli@fbk.eu

Jesper Hoeksema
The Network Institute
VU University Amsterdam
j.e.hoeksema@vu.nl

Abstract

This paper introduces GAF, a grounded annotation framework to represent events in a formal context that can represent information from both textual and extra-textual sources. GAF makes a clear distinction between *mentions* of events in text and their formal representation as *instances* in a **semantic layer**. Instances are represented by RDF compliant URIs that are shared across different research disciplines. This allows us to complete textual information with external sources and facilitates reasoning. The semantic layer can integrate any linguistic information and is compatible with previous event representations in NLP. Through a use case on earthquakes in Southeast Asia, we demonstrate GAF flexibility and ability to reason over events with the aid of extra-linguistic resources.

1 Introduction

Events are not only described in textual documents, they are also represented in many other non-textual sources. These sources include videos, pictures, sensors or evidence from data registration such as mobile phone data, financial transactions and hospital registrations. Nevertheless, many approaches to textual event annotation consider events as text-internal-affairs, possibly across multiple documents but seldom across different modalities. It follows from the above that event representation is not exclusively a concern for the NLP community. It also plays a major role in several other branches of information science such as knowledge representation and the Semantic Web, which have created their own models for representing events.

We propose a grounded annotation framework (GAF) that allows us to interconnect different ways of describing and registering events, including non-linguistic sources. GAF representations can be used to reason over the cumulated and linked sources of knowledge and information to interpret the often incomplete and fragmented information that is provided by each source. We make a clear distinction between *mentions* of events in text or any other form of registration and their formal representation as *instances* in a **semantic layer**.

Mentions in text are annotated using the Terence Annotation Format (Moens et al., 2011, TAF) on top of which the semantic layer is realized using Semantic Web technologies and standards. In this semantic layer, instances are denoted with Uniform Resource Identifiers (URIs). Attributes and relations are expressed according to the Simple Event Model (Van Hage et al., 2011, SEM) and other established ontologies. Statements are grouped in named graphs based on provenance and (temporal) validity, enabling the representation of conflicting information. External knowledge can be related to instances from a wide variety of sources such as those found in the Linked Open Data Cloud (Bizer et al., 2009a).

Instances in the semantic layer can optionally be linked to one or more mentions in text or to other sources. Because linking instances is optional, our representation offers a straightforward way to include information that can be inferred from text, such as implied participants or whether an event is part of a series that is not explicitly mentioned. Due to the fact that each URI is unique, it is clear that mentions connected to the same URI have a coreferential relation. Other relations between instances (participants, subevents, temporal relations, etc.) are represented explicitly in the semantic layer.

The remainder of this paper is structured as follows. In Section 2, we present related work and explain the motivation behind our approach. Section 3 describes the in-text annotation approach. Our semantic annotation layer is presented in Section 4. Sections 5-7 present GAF through a use case on earthquakes in Indonesia. This is followed by our conclusions and future work in section 8.

2 Motivation and Background

Annotation of events and of relations between them has a long tradition in NLP. The MUC conferences (Grishman and Sundheim, 1996) in the 90s did not explicitly annotate events and coreference relations, but the templates used for evaluating the information extraction tasks indirectly can be seen as annotation of events represented in newswires. Such events are not ordered in time or further related to each other. In response, Setzer and Gaizauskas (2000) describe an annotation framework to create coherent temporal orderings of events represented in documents using closure rules. They suggest that reasoning with text independent models, such as a calendar, helps annotating textual representations.

More recently, generic corpora, such as Propbank (Palmer et al., 2005) and the Framenet corpus (Baker et al., 2003) have been built according to linguistic principles. The annotations aim at properly representing verb structures within a sentence context, focusing on verb arguments, semantic roles and other elements. In ACE 2004 (Linguistic Data Consortium, 2004b), event detection and linking is included as a pilot task for the first time, inspired by annotation schemes developed for named entities. They distinguish between event mentions and the trigger event, which is the mention that most clearly expresses its occurrence (Linguistic Data Consortium, 2004a). Typically, agreement on the trigger event is low across annotators (around 55% (Moens et al., 2011)). Timebank (Pustejovsky et al., 2006b) is a more recent corpus for representing events and time-expressions that includes temporal relations in addition to plain coreference relations.

All these approaches have in common that they consider the textual representation as a closed world within which events need to be represented. This means that mentions are linked to a trigger event or to each other but not to an independent semantic representation. More recently, researchers started to annotate events across multiple documents, such as the EventCorefBank (Bejan and Harabagiu, 2010). Cross-document coreference is more challenging for establishing the trigger event, but it is in essence not different from annotating textual event coreference within a single document. Descriptions of events across documents may complement each other providing a more complete picture, but still textual descriptions tend to be incomplete and sparse with respect to time, place and participants. At the same time, the comparison of events becomes more complex. We thus expect even lower agreement in assigning trigger events across documents. Nothman et al. (2012) define the trigger as the first new article that mentions an event, which is easier than to find the clearest description and still report inter-annotator agreement of .48 and .73, respectively.

Recent approaches to automatically resolve event coreference (cf. Chambers and Jurafsky (2011a), Bejan and Harabagiu (2010)) use some background data to establish coreference and other relations between events in text. Background information, including resources, and models learned from textual data do not represent mentions of events directly but are useful to fill gaps of knowledge in the textual descriptions. They do not alter the model for annotation as such.

We aim to take these recent efforts one step further and propose a grounded annotation framework (GAF). Our main goal is to integrate information from text analysis in a **formal context** shared with researchers across domains. Furthermore, GAF is **flexible** enough to contain contradictory information. This is both important to represent sources that (partially) contradict each other and to combine alternative annotations or output of different NLP tools. Because conflicting information may be present, **provenance** of information is provided in our framework, so that we may decide which source to trust more or use it as a feature to decide which interpretation to follow. Different models of event representation exist that can contribute valuable information. Therefore our model is compliant with prior approaches regardless of whether they are manual or automatic. Finally, GAF makes a clear distinction between *instances* and *instance mentions* avoiding the problem of determining a trigger event. Additionally, it facilitates the integration of information from extra-textual sources and information that can be inferred from texts, but is not explicitly mentioned. Sections 5 to 7 will explain how we can achieve this with GAF.

3 The TERENCE annotation format

The TERENCE Annotation Format (TAF) is defined within the TERENCE Project[1] with the goal to include event mentions, temporal expressions and participant mentions in a single annotation protocol (Moens et al., 2011). TAF is based on ISO-TimeML (Pustejovsky et al., 2010), but introduces several adaptations in order to fit the domain of children's stories for which it was originally developed. The format has been used to annotate around 30 children stories in Italian and 10 in English.

We selected TAF as the basis for our in-text annotation for three reasons. First, it incorporates the (in our opinion crucial) distinction between *instances* and *instance mentions*. Second, it adapts some consolidated paradigms for linguistic annotation such as TimeML for events and temporal expressions and ACE for participants and participant mentions (Linguistic Data Consortium, 2005). It is thus compatible with other annotation schemes. Third, it integrates the annotation of event mentions, participants and temporal expressions into a unified framework. We will elaborate briefly on these properties below.

As mentioned, TAF makes a clear distinction between *instances* and *instance mentions*. Originally, this distinction only applied to nominal and named entities, similar to ACE (Linguistic Data Consortium, 2005), because children's stories can generally be treated as a closed world, usually presenting a simple sequence of events that do not corefer. Event coreference and linking to other sources was thus not relevant for this domain. In GAF, we extend the distinction between instances and instance mentions to events to model event coreference, link them to other sources and create a consistent model for all instances.

Children's stories usually include a small set of characters, event sequences (mostly in chronological order), and a few generic temporal expressions. In the TERENCE project, modeling characters in the stories is necessary. This requires an extension of TimeML to deal with event participants. Pustejovsky et al. (2006a) address the need to include arguments in TimeML annotations, but that proposal did not include specific examples and details on how to perform annotation (e.g., on the participants' attributes). Such guidelines were created for TAF.

The TAF annotation of *event mentions* largely follows TimeML in annotating tense, aspect, class, mood, modality and polarity and temporal expressions. However, there are several differences between TAF and TimeML. First, temporal expressions are not normalized into the ISO-8601 form, because most children's stories are not fixed to a specific date. In GAF, the normalization of expressions takes place in the semantic layer as these go beyond the scope of the text. As a result, temporal vagueness of linguistic expressions in text do not need to be normalized in the textual representation to actual time points and remain underspecified.[2]

In TAF, events and participant mentions are linked through a *has_participant* relation, which is defined as a directional, one-to-one relation from the event to the participant mentions. Only mentions corresponding to mandatory arguments of the events in the story are annotated. Annotators look up each verb in a reference dictionary providing information on the predicate-argument structure of each verb. This makes annotation easier and generally not controversial. However, this kind of information can be provided only by annotators having a good knowledge of linguistics.

All annotations are performed with the Celct An-

[1] ICT FP7 Programme, ICT-2010-25410, `http://www.terenceproject.eu/`

[2] Note that we can still use existing tools for normalization at the linguistic level: early normalizations can be integrated in the semantic layer alongside normalizations carried out at a later point.

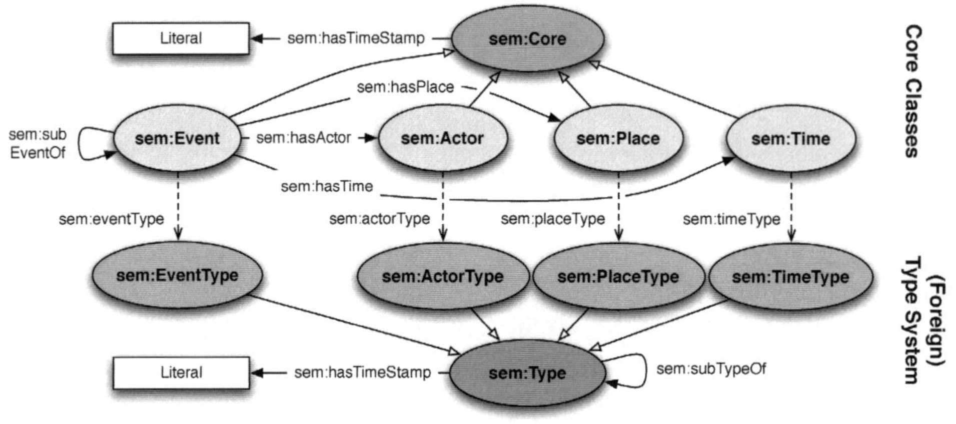

Figure 1: The SEM ontology

notation Tool (Bartalesi Lenzi et al., 2012), an online tool supporting TimeML that can easily be extended to include participant information. The annotated file can be exported to various XML formats and imported into the semantic layer. The next section describes SEM, the event model used in our semantic layer, and how it complements the TAF annotations.

4 The Simple Event Model

The Simple Event Model (SEM) is an RDF schema (Carroll and Klyne, 2004; Guha and Brickley, 2004) to express *who* did *what*, *where*, and *when*. There are many RDF schemas and OWL ontologies (Motik et al., 2009) that describe events, e.g., Shaw et al. (2009), Crofts et al. (2008) and Scherp et al. (2009). SEM is among the most flexible and easiest to adapt to different domains. SEM describes events and related instances such as the place, time and participants (called Actors in SEM) by representing the interactions between the instances with RDF triples. SEM models are semantic networks that include events, places, times, participants and all related concepts, such as their types.

An overview of all the classes in the SEM ontology and the relations connecting them is shown in Figure 1. Nodes can be identified by URIs, which universally identify them across all RDF models. If for example one uses the URI used by DBpedia[3] (Bizer et al., 2009b) for the 2004 catastrophe in Indonesia, then one really means the same event as everybody else who uses that URI. SEM does not put any constraints on the RDF vocabulary, so vocabularies can easily be reused. Places and place types can for example be imported from GeoNames[4] and event types from the RDF version of WordNet.

SEM supports two types of abstraction: generalization with hierarchical relations from other ontologies, such as the subclass relation from RDFS, and aggregation of events into superevents with the `sem:subEventOf` relation, as exemplified in Figure 2. Other types of abstractions can be represented using additional schemas or ontologies in combination with SEM. For instance, temporal aggregation can be done with constructs from the OWL Time ontology (Hobbs and Pan, 2004).

Relations between events and other instances, which could be other events, places, actors, times, or external concepts, can be modeled using the `sem:eventProperty` relation. This relation can be refined to represent specific relations, such as specific participation, causality or simultaneity relations. The provenance of information in the SEM graph is captured through assigning contexts to statements using the PROV Data Model (Moreau et al., 2012). In this manner, all statements derived from a specific newspaper article are stored in a named graph that represents that origin. Conflicting statements can be stored in different named graphs, and can thus coexist. This gives us the possibility

[3] `http://dbpedia.org`

[4] `http://www.geonames.org/ontology/`

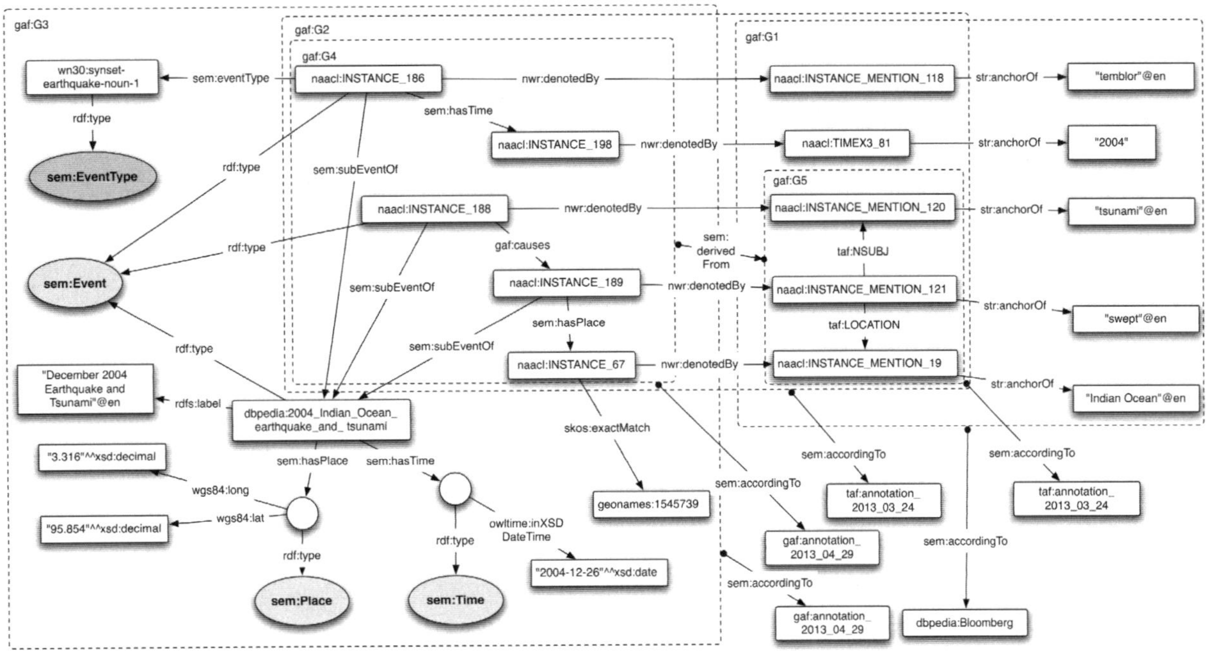

Figure 2: Partial SEM representation of December 26th 2004 Earthquake

of delaying or ignoring the resolution of the conflict, which enables use cases that require the analysis of the conflict itself.

5 The GAF Annotation Framework

This section explains the basic idea behind GAF by using texts on earthquakes in Indonesia. GAF provides a general model for event representation (including textual and extra-textual mentions) as well as exact representation of linguistic annotation or output of NLP tools. Simply put, GAF is the combination of textual analyses and formal semantic representations in RDF.

5.1 A SEM for earthquakes

We selected newspaper texts on the January 2009 West Papua earthquakes from Bejan and Harabagiu (2010) to illustrate GAF. This choice was made because the topic "earthquake" illustrates the advantage of sharing URIs across domains. Gao and Hunter (2011) propose a Linked Data model to capture major geological events such as earthquakes, volcano activity and tsunamis. They combine information from different seismological databases with the intention to provide more complete information to experts which may help to predict the occurrence of such events. The information can also be used in text interpretation. We can verify whether interpretations by NLP tools correspond to the data and relations defined by geologists or, through generalization, which interpretation is the most sensible given what we know about the events. General information on events obtained from automatic text processing, such as event templates (Chambers and Jurafsky, 2011b) or typical event durations (Gusev et al., 2010) can be integrated in SEM in a similar manner. Provenance indications can be used to indicate whether information is based on a model created by an expert or an automatically derived model obtained by a particular approach.

Figure 2 provides a fragment of a SEM representation for the earthquake and tsunami of December 26 2004.[5] The model is partially inspired by Gao and Hunter (2011)'s proposal. It combines information extracted from texts with information from DBpedia. The linking between the two can be established either manually or automatically through

[5]The annotation and a larger representation including the sentence it represents can be found on the GAF website `http://wordpress.let.vu.nl/gaf`.

an entity linking system.[6] The combined event of the earthquake and tsunami is represented by a DBpedia URI. The node labeled naacl:INSTANCE_186 represents the earthquake itself. The unambiguous representation of the 2004 earthquake leads us to additional information about it, for instance that the earthquake is an event (`sem:Event`) and that the `sem:EventType` is an earthquake, in this case represented by a synset from WordNet, but also the exact date it occurred and the exact location (cf `sem:hasTime, sem:hasPlace`).

5.2 Integrating TAF representations into SEM

TAF annotations are converted to SEM relations. For example, the TAF `as_participant` relations are translated to `sem:hasActor` relations, and temporal relations are translated to `sem:hasTime`. We use the relation `nwr:denotedBy` to link instances to their mentions in the text which are represented by their unique identifiers in Figure 2.

Named graphs are used to model the source of information as discussed in Section 4. The relation `sem:accordingTo` indicates provenance of information in the graph.[7] For instance, the mentions from the text in named graph `gaf:G1` come from the source `dbpedia:Bloomberg`. Relations between instances (e.g. between INSTANCE_189 and INSTANCE_188) are derived from a specific grammatical relation in the text (here, that *tsunami* is subject of *swept*) indicated by the `nwr:derivedFrom` relation from `gaf:G5` to `gaf:G4`. The grammatical relations included in graph `gaf:G5` come from a TAF annotation (`tag:annotation_2013_03_24`).

6 GAF Earthquake Examples

This section takes a closer look at a few selected sentences from the text that illustrate different aspects of GAF. Figure 2 showed how a URI can provide a **formal context** including important background information on the event. Several texts in the corpus refer to the tsunami of December 26, 2004, *a 9.1 temblor in 2004 caused a tsunami* and *The catastrophe four years ago*, among others. Compared to time expressions such as *2004* and *four years ago*, time indications extracted from external sources like DBpedia are not only more precise, but also permit us to correctly establish the fact that these expressions refer to the same event and thus indicate the same time. The articles were published in January 2009: a direct normalization of time indications would have placed the catastrophe in 2005. The **flexibility** to combine these seemingly conflicting time indications and delay normalization can be used to correctly interpret that *four years ago* early January 2009 refers to an event taking place at the end of December 2004.

A fragment relating to one of the earthquakes of January 2009: *The quake struck off the coast [...] 75 kilometers (50 miles) west of [....] Manokwari* provides a similar example. The expressions *75 kilometers* and *50 miles* are clearly meant to express the same distance, but not identical. The location is most likely neither exactly 75 km nor 50 miles. SEM can represent an underspecified location that is included in the correct region. The exact location of the earthquake can be found in external resources. We can include both distances as expressions of the location and decide whether they denote the general location or include the normalized locations as alternatives to those from external resources.

Different sources may report different details. Details may only be known later, or sources may report from a different perspective. As **provenance** information can be incorporated into the semantic layer, we can represent different perspectives, and choose which one to use when reasoning over the information. For example, the following phrases indicate the magnitude of the earthquakes that struck Manokwari on January 4, 2009:

the 7.7 magnitude quake (source: Xinhuanet)
two quakes, measuring 7.6 and 7.4 (source: Bloomberg)
One 7.3-magnitude tremor (source: Jakartapost)

The first two magnitude indicators (7.7, 7.6) are likely to pertain to the same earthquake, just as the second two (7.4, 7.3) are. Trust indicators can be found through the provenance trace of each men-

[6] Entity linking is the task of associating a mention to an instance in a knowledge base. Several approaches and tools for entity linking w.r.t. DBpedia and other data sets in the Linked Open Data cloud are available and achieve good performances, such as DBpedia Spotlight (Mendes et al., 2011); see (Rizzo and Troncy, 2011) for a comparison of tools.

[7] The use of named graphs in this way to denote context is compatible with the method used by Bozzato et al. (2012).

tion. Trust indicators can include the date on which it was published, properties of the creation process, the author, or publisher (Ceolin et al., 2010). Furthermore, because the URIs are shared across domains, we can link the information from the text to information from seismological databases, which may contain the exact measurement for the quake.

Similarly, external information obtained through shared links can help us establish coreference. Consider the sentences in Figure 3. There are several ways to establish that the same event is meant in all three sentences by using shared URIs and reasoning. All sentences give us approximate time indications, location of the affected area and casualties. Reasoning over these sentences combined with external knowledge allows us to infer facts such as that *undersea [...] off [...] Aceh* will be in the Indian Ocean, or that the affected countries listed in the first sentence are *countries around the Indian Ocean*, which constitutes the *Indian Ocean Community*. The number of casualties in combination of the approximate time indication or approximate location suffices to identify the earthquake and tsunami in Indonesia on December 26, 2004. The DBpedia representation contains additional information such as the magnitude, exact location of the quake and a list of affected countries, which can be used for additional verification. This example illustrates how a **formal context** using URIs that are shared across disciplines of information science can help to determine exact referents from limited or imprecise information.

7 Creating GAF

GAF entails integrating linguistic information (e.g. TAF annotations) into RDF models (e.g. SEM). The information in the model includes **provenance** that points back to specific annotations. There are two approaches to annotate text according to GAF. The first approach is bottom-up. Mentions are marked in the text as well as relations between them (participants, time, causal relations, basically anything except coreference). Consequently, these annotations are converted to SEM representations as explained above. Coreference is established by linking mentions to the same instance in SEM. The second approach is top-down. Here, annotators mark relations between instances (events, their participants, time relations, etc.) directly into SEM and then link these to mentions in the text.

As mention in Section 2, inter-annotator agreement on event annotation is generally low showing that it is challenging. The task is somewhat simplified in GAF, since it removes the problem of identifying an event trigger in the text. The GAF equivalent of the event trigger in other linguistic annotation approaches is an instance in SEM. However, other challenges such as which mentions to select are in principle not addressed by GAF, though differences in inter-annotator agreement may be found depending on whether the bottom-up approach or the top-down approach is selected. The formal context of SEM may help frame annotations, especially for domains such as earthquakes, where expert knowledge was used to create basic event models. This may help annotators while defining the correct relations between events. On the other hand, the top-down approach may lead to additional challenges, because annotators are forced to link events to unambiguous instances leading to hesitations as to when new instances should be introduced.

Currently, we only use the bottom-up approach. The main reason is the lack of an appropriate annotation tool to directly annotate information in SEM. We plan to perform comparative studies between the two annotation approaches in future work.

8 Conclusion and Future Work

We presented GAF, an event annotation framework in which textual mentions of events are grounded in a semantic model that facilitates linking these events to mentions in external (possibly non-textual) resources and thereby reasoning. We illustrated how GAF combines TAF and SEM through a use case on earthquakes. We explained that we aim for a representation that can combine textual and extra-linguistic information, provides a clear distinction between instances and instance mentions, is flexible enough to include conflicting information and clearly marks the provenance of information.

GAF ticks all these boxes. All instances are represented by URIs in a semantic layer following standard RDF representations that are shared across research disciplines. They are thus represented completely independent of the source and clearly distin-

```
There have been hundreds of earthquakes in Indonesia since a 9.1 temblor in 2004 caused a
tsunami that swept across the Indian Ocean, devastating coastal communities and leaving more
than 220,000 people dead in Indonesia, Sri Lanka, India, Thailand and other countries.
(Bloomberg, 2009-01-07 01:55 EST)

The catastrophe four years ago devastated Indian Ocean community and killed more than 230,000
people, over 170,000 of them in Aceh at northern tip of Sumatra Island of Indonesia.
(Xinhuanet, 2009-01-05 13:25:46 GMT)

In December 2004, a massive undersea quake off the western Indonesian province of Aceh
triggered a giant tsunami that left at least 230,000 people dead and missing in a dozen
countries facing the Indian Ocean.  (Aljazeera, 2009-01-05 08:49 GMT)
```

Figure 3: Sample sentences mentioning the December 2004 Indonesian earthquake from sample texts

guished from mentions in text or mentions in other sources. The Terence Annotation Format (TAF) provides a unified framework to annotate events, participants and temporal expressions (and the corresponding relations) by leaning on past, consolidated annotation experiences such TimeML and ACE. We will harmonize TAF, the Kyoto Annotation Format (Bosma et al., 2009, KAF) and the NLP Interchange Format (Hellmann et al., 2012, NIF) with respect to the textual representation in the near future. The NAF format includes the lessons learned from these predecessors: layered standoff representations using URI as identifiers and where possible standardized data categories. The formal semantic model (SEM) provides the flexibility to include conflicting information as well as indications of the provenance of this information. This allows us to use inferencing and reasoning over the cumulated and aggregated information, possibly exploiting the provenance of the type of information source. This flexibility also makes our representation compatible with all approaches dealing with event representation and detections mentioned in Section 2. It can include automatically learned templates as well as specific relations between events and time expressed in text. Moreover, it may simultaneously contain output of different NLP tools.

The proposed semantic layer may be simple, its flexibility in importing external knowledge may increase complexity in usage as it can model events in every thinkable domain. To resolve this issue, it is important to scope the domain by importing the appropriate vocabularies, but no more. When keeping this in mind, reasoning with SEM is shown to be rich but still versatile (Van Hage et al., 2012).

While GAF provides us with the desired granularity and flexibility for the event annotation tasks we envision, a thorough evaluation still needs to be carried out. This includes an evaluation of the annotations created with GAF compared to other annotation formats, as well as testing it within a greater application. A comparative study of top-down and bottom-up annotation will also be carried out. As already mentioned in Section 7, there is no appropriate modeling tool for SEM yet. We are currently using the CAT tool to create TAF annotations and convert those to SEM, but will develop a tool to annotate the semantic layer directly for this comparative study.

The most interesting effect of the GAF annotations is that it provides us with relatively simple access to a vast wealth of extra-linguistic information, which we can utilize in a variety of NLP tasks; some of the reasoning options that are made available by the pairing up with Semantic Web technology may for example aid us in identifying coreference relations between events. Investigating the implications of this combination of NLP and Semantic Web technologies lies at the heart of our future work.

Acknowledgements

We thank Francesco Corcoglioniti for his helpful comments and suggestions. The research leading to this paper was supported by the European Union's 7th Framework Programme via the NewsReader Project (ICT-316404) and by the BiographyNed project, funded by the Netherlands eScience Center (http://esciencecenter.nl/). Partners in BiographyNed are Huygens/ING Institute of the Dutch Academy of Sciences and VU University Amsterdam.

References

Collin F. Baker, Charles J. Fillmore, and Beau Cronin. 2003. The structure of the FrameNet database. *International Journal of Lexicography*, 16(3):281–296.

Valentina Bartalesi Lenzi, Giovanni Moretti, and Rachele Sprugnoli. 2012. CAT: the CELCT Annotation Tool. In *Proceedings of LREC 2012*.

Cosmin Bejan and Sandra Harabagiu. 2010. Unsupervised event coreference resolution with rich linguistic features. In *Proceedings of the 48th Annual Meeting of the Association for Computational Linguistics*, pages 1412–1422.

Christian Bizer, Tom Heath, and Tim Berners-Lee. 2009a. Linked data - the story so far. *International Journal on Semantic Web and Information Systems*, 5(3):1–22.

Christian Bizer, Jens Lehmann, Georgi Kobilarov, Sören Auer, Christian Becker, Richard Cyganiak, and Sebastian Hellmann. 2009b. DBpedia - A crystallization point for the Web of Data. *Web Semantics: Science, Services and Agents on the World Wide Web*, 7(3):154 – 165.

Wauter Bosma, Piek Vossen, Aitor Soroa, German Rigau, Maurizio Tesconi, Andrea Marchetti, Monica Monachini, and Carlo Aliprandi. 2009. KAF: a generic semantic annotation format. In *Proceedings of the 5th International Conference on Generative Approaches to the Lexicon GL 2009*, Pisa, Italy.

Loris Bozzato, Francesco Corcoglioniti, Martin Homola, Mathew Joseph, and Luciano Serafini. 2012. Managing contextualized knowledge with the ckr (poster). In *Proceedings of the 9th Extended Semantic Web Conference (ESWC 2012)*, May 27-31.

Jeremy J. Carroll and Graham Klyne. 2004. Resource description framework (RDF): Concepts and abstract syntax. W3C recommendation, W3C, February. http://www.w3.org/TR/2004/REC-rdf-concepts-20040210/.

Davide Ceolin, Paul Groth, and Willem Robert Van Hage. 2010. Calculating the trust of event descriptions using provenance. *Proceedings Of The SWPM*.

Nathanael Chambers and Dan Jurafsky. 2011a. Template-based information extraction without the templates. In *Proceedings of ACL-2011*.

Nathanael Chambers and Dan Jurafsky. 2011b. Template-based information extraction without the templates. In *Proceedings of ACL-2011*, Portland, OR.

Nick Crofts, Martin Doerr, Tony Gill, Stephen Stead, and Matthew Stiff. 2008. Definition of the CIDOC Conceptual Reference Model. Technical report, ICOM/CIDOC CRM Special Interest Group. version 4.2.5.

Lianli Gao and Jane Hunter. 2011. Publishing, linking and annotating events via interactive timelines: an earth sciences case study. In *DeRiVE 2011 (Detection, Representation, and Exploitation of Events in the Semantic Web) Workshop in conjunction with ISWC 2011*, Bonn, Germany.

Ralph Grishman and Beth Sundheim. 1996. Message understanding conference - 6: A brief history. In *Proceedings of the 16th conference on Computational linguistics (COLING'96)*, pages 466–471.

Ramanathan V. Guha and Dan Brickley. 2004. RDF vocabulary description language 1.0: RDF schema. W3C recommendation, W3C, February. http://www.w3.org/TR/2004/REC-rdf-schema-20040210/.

Andrey Gusev, Nathanael Chambers, Pranav Khaitan, Divye Khilnani, Steven Bethard, and Dan Jurafsky. 2010. Using query patterns to learn the duration of events. In *Proceedings of ISWC 2010*.

Sebastian Hellmann, Jens Lehmann, and Sören Auer. 2012. NIF: An ontology-based and linked-data-aware NLP Interchange Format. Working Draft.

Jerry R Hobbs and Feng Pan. 2004. An ontology of time for the semantic web. *ACM Transactions on Asian Language Information Processing (TALIP)*, 3(1):66–85.

Linguistic Data Consortium. 2004a. Annotation Guidelines for Event Detection and Characterization (EDC). `http://projects.ldc.upenn.edu/ace/docs/EnglishEDCV2.0.pdf`.

Linguistic Data Consortium. 2004b. The ACE 2004 Evaluation Plan. Technical report, LDC.

Linguistic Data Consortium. 2005. ACE (Automatic Content Extraction) English annotation guidelines for entities. Version 6.6, July.

Pablo N. Mendes, Max Jakob, Andrés García-Silva, and Christian Bizer. 2011. Dbpedia spotlight: shedding light on the web of documents. In *Proceedings of the 7th International Conference on Semantic Systems*, I-Semantics '11, pages 1–8.

Marie-Francine Moens, Oleksandr Kolomiyets, Emanuele Pianta, Sara Tonelli, and Steven Bethard. 2011. D3.1: State-of-the-art and design of novel annotation languages and technologies: Updated version. Technical report, TERENCE project – ICT FP7 Programme – ICT-2010-25410.

Luc Moreau, Paolo Missier, Khalid Belhajjame, Reza B'Far, James Cheney, Sam Coppens, Stephen Cresswell, Yolanda Gil, Paul Groth, Graham Klyne, Timothy Lebo, Jim McCusker, Simon Miles, James Myers, Satya Sahoo, and Curt Tilmes. 2012. PROV-DM: The PROV Data Model. Technical report.

Boris Motik, Bijan Parsia, and Peter F. Patel-Schneider. 2009. OWL 2 Web Ontology

Language structural specification and functional-style syntax. W3C recommendation, W3C, October. `http://www.w3.org/TR/2009/REC-owl2-syntax-20091027/`.

Joel Nothman, Matthew Honnibal, Ben Hachey, and James R. Curran. 2012. Event linking: Grounding event reference in a news archive. In *Proceedings of the 50th Annual Meeting of the Association for Computational Linguistics (Volume 2: Short Papers)*, pages 228–232, Jeju Island, Korea, July. Association for Computational Linguistics.

Martha Palmer, Daniel Gildea, and Paul Kingsbury. 2005. The proposition bank: An annotated corpus of semantic roles. *Computational Linguistics*, 31(1):71–106, 2013/03/12.

James Pustejovsky, Jessica Littman, and Roser Saurì. 2006a. Argument Structure in TimeML. In *Dagstuhl Seminar Proceedings. Internationales Begegnungs- und Forschungszentrum.*

James Pustejovsky, Jessica Littman, Roser Saurí, and Marc Verhagen. 2006b. Timebank 1.2 documentation. Technical report, Brandeis University, April.

James Pustejovsky, Kiyong Lee, Harry Bunt, and Laurent Romary. 2010. ISO-TimeML: An international standard for semantic annotation. In *Proceedings o the Fifth International Workshop on Interoperable Semantic Annotation.*

Giuseppe Rizzo and Raphaël Troncy. 2011. NERD: A framework for evaluating named entity recognition tools in the Web of data. In *Workshop on Web Scale Knowledge Extraction, colocated with ISWC 2011.*

Ansgar Scherp, Thomas Franz, Carsten Saathoff, and Steffen Staab. 2009. F–a model of events based on the foundational ontology dolce+ dns ultralight. In *Proceedings of the fifth international conference on Knowledge capture*, pages 137–144. ACM.

Andrea Setzer and Robert J. Gaizauskas. 2000. Annotating events and temporal information in newswire texts. In *LREC*. European Language Resources Association.

Ryan Shaw, Raphaël Troncy, and Lynda Hardman. 2009. LODE: Linking Open Descriptions of Events. In *4th Annual Asian Semantic Web Conference (ASWC'09)*, Shanghai, China.

Willem Robert Van Hage, Véronique Malaisé, Roxane Segers, Laura Hollink, and Guus Schreiber. 2011. Design and use of the simple event model (SEM). *Journal of Web Semantics.*

Willem Robert Van Hage, Marieke Van Erp, and Véronique Malaisé. 2012. Linked open piracy: A story about e-science, linked data, and statistics. *Journal on Data Semantics*, 1(3):187–201.

Events are Not Simple: Identity, Non-Identity, and Quasi-Identity

Eduard Hovy
Language Technology Institute
Carnegie Mellon University
5000 Forbes Avenue
Pittsburgh, PA 15213, USA
hovy@cmu.edu

Teruko Mitamura
Language Technology Institute
Carnegie Mellon University
5000 Forbes Avenue
Pittsburgh, PA 15213, USA
teruko@cs.cmu.edu

Felisa Verdejo
E.T.S.I. Informática, UNED
C/ Juan del Rosal, 16
(Ciudad Universitaria)
28040 Madrid, Spain
felisa@lsi.uned.es

Jun Araki
Language Technology Institute
Carnegie Mellon University
5000 Forbes Avenue
Pittsburgh, PA 15213, USA
junaraki@cs.cmu.edu

Andrew Philpot
Information Sciences Institute
University of Southern California
4676 Admiralty Way
Marina del Rey, CA 90292, USA
philpot@isi.edu

Abstract[1]

Despite considerable theoretical and computational work on coreference, deciding when two entities or events are identical is very difficult. In a project to build corpora containing coreference links between events, we have identified three levels of event identity (full, partial, and none). Event coreference annotation on two corpora was performed to validate the findings.

1 The Problem of Identity

Last year we had HLT in Montreal, and this year we did it in Atlanta.

Does the "did it" refer to the same conference or a different one? The two conferences are not identical, of course, but they are also not totally unrelated—else the "did it" would not be interpretable.

When creating text, we treat instances of entities and events as if they are fixed, well-described, and well-understood. When we say "that boat over there" or "Mary's wedding next month", we assume the reader creates a mental representation of the referent, and we proceed to refer to it without further thought.

However, as has been often noted in theoretical studies of semantics, this assumption is very problematic (Mill, 1872; Frege 1892; Guarino, 1999). Entities and (even more so) events are complex composite phenomena in the world, and they undergo change.

Since nobody has complete knowledge, the author's mental image of the entity or event in question might differ from the reader's, and from the truth. Specifically, the properties the author assumes for the event or entity might not be the ones the reader assumes. This difference has deep consequences for the treatment of the semantic meaning of a text. In particular, it fundamentally affects how one must perform coreference among entities or events.

As discussed in Section 6, events have been the focus of study in both Linguistics and NLP (Chen and Ji, 2009; Bejan and Harabagiu, 2008, 2010; Humphreys et al., 1997). Determining when two event mentions in text corefer is, however, an unsolved problem[2]. Past work in NLP has avoided some of the more complex problems by considering only certain types of coreference, or by simply ignoring the major problems. The results have been partial, or inconsistent, annotations.

In this paper we describe our approach to the problem of coreference among events. In order to build a corpus containing event coreference links that is annotated with high enough inter-annotator agreement to be useful for machine learning, it has proven necessary to create a model of event identity that is more elaborate than is usually assumed in the NLP literature, and to formulate quite specific definitions for its central concepts.

---

[1] This work was supported by grants from DARPA and NSF, as well as by funding that supported Prof. M. Felisa Vedejo from UNED Madrid.

[2] In this work, we mean both events and states when we say "event". A state refers to a fixed, or regularly changing, configuration of entities in the world, such as "it is hot" or "he is running". An event occurs when there is a change of state in the world, such as "he stops running" or "the plane took off".

Event coreference is the problem of determining when two mentions in a text refer to the 'same' event. Whether or not the event actually occurred in reality is a separate issue; a text can describe people flying around on dragons or broomsticks. While the events might be actual occurrences, hypothesized or desired ones, etc., they exist in the text as *Discourse Elements* (DEs), and this is what we consider in this work.

Each DE is referred to (explicitly or implicitly) in the text by a *mention*, for example "destroy", "the attack", "that event", or "it". But it is often unclear whether two mentions refer to the same DE or to closely related ones, or to something altogether different. The following example illustrates two principal problems of event coreference:

> While Turkish troops have been **fighting_E.1** a Kurdish faction in northern Iraq, two other Kurdish groups have been **battling_E.2** each other.
>
> A radio station **operated_E.3** by the Kurdistan Democratic Party **said_E.4** the party's forces **attacked_E.5** positions of the Patriotic Union of Kurdistan on Monday in the Kurdish region's capital Irbil.
>
> The Voice of Iraqi Kurdistan radio, **monitored_E.6** by the British Broadcasting Corp., **said_E.7** more than 80 Patriotic Union fighters **were killed_E.8** and at least 150 **wounded_E.9**.
>
> The **fighting_E.10** was also **reported_E.11** by a senior Patriotic Union official, Kusret Rasul Ali, who **said_E.12** PUK forces **repelled_E.13** a large KDP **attack_E.14**.
>
> ...
>
> Ali **claimed_E.16** that 300 KDP fighters were **killed_E.17** or **wounded_E.18** and only 11 Patriotic Union members **died_E.19**.

Problem 1: Partial event overlap. Event E.2, "battling each other", refers to an ongoing series of skirmishes between two Kurdish groups, the KDP and the PUK. Since one of these battles, where the KDP attacked positions of the PUK, is E.5, it is natural to say that E.2 and E.5 corefer. However, E.2 clearly denotes other battles as well, and therefore E.5 and E.2 cannot fully corefer. In another example, event E.8 refers to the killing of a number of soldiers as part of this fight E.5, and event E.9 to the wounding of others. Both events E.8 and E.9 constitute an intrinsic part of the attack E.5, and hence corefer to it, but are each only part of E.5, and hence neither can fully corefer to it.

Problem 2: Inconsistent reporting. This news fragment contains two reports of the fight: E.5 and E.10. Since E.10 describes E.5 from the perspective of a senior PUK official, it should corefer to E.5. But where the KDP's report claims more than 80 PUK fighters killed (event E.8, part of E.5), the PUK official said that only 11 PUK members died (event E.19, part of E.10). Without taking into account the fact that the two killing events are reports made by different speakers, it would not be possible to recognize them as coreferent.

Examples of partial event overlap and inconsistent reporting are common in text, and occur as various types. In our work, we formally recognize partial event overlap, calling it *partial event identity*, which permits different degrees and types of event coreference. This approach simplifies the coreference problem and highlights various inter-event relationships that facilitates grouping events into 'families' that support further analysis and combination with other NLP system components.

In this paper, we introduce the idea that there are three degrees of event identity: fully identical, quasi-identical, and fully independent (not identical). Full identity reflects in full coreference and quasi-identity in partial coreference. Fully independent events are singletons.

Our claims in this paper are:

- Events, being complex phenomena, can corefer fully (identity) or partially (quasi-identity).
- Event coreference annotation is considerably clarified when partial coreference is allowed.
- A relatively small fixed set of types of quasi-identity suffices to describe most of them.
- Different domains and genres highlight different subsets of these quasi-identity types.
- Different auxiliary knowledge sources and texts are relevant for different types.

2 Types of Full and Partial Identity

Def: Two mentions **fully corefer** if their activity/event/state DE is identical in all respects, as far as one can tell from their occurrence in the text. (In particular, their agents, location, and time are identical or compatible.) One can distinguish several types of identity, as spelled out below.

Def: Two mentions **partially corefer** if activity/event/state DE is quasi-identical: most aspects are the same, but some additional information is provided for one or the other that is not shared. There are two principal types of quasi-identity, as defined below.

Otherwise, two mentions **do not corefer**.

2.1 Full Identity

Mention1 is identical to mention2 iff there is no semantic (meaning) difference between them. Just one DE, and exactly the same aspects of the DE, are understood from both mentions in their contexts. It is possible to replace the one mention with the other without any semantic change (though some small syntactic changes might be required to ensure grammaticality). Note that mention2 may contain less detail than mention1 and remain identical, if it carries over information from mention1 that is understood / inherited from the context. However, when mention2 provides more or new information not contained in mention1 or naturally inferred for it, then the two are no longer identical. Usually, exact identity is rare within a single text, but may occur more often across texts. We identify the following types:

1. **Lexical identity**: The two mentions use exactly the same senses of the same word(s), including derivational words (e.g., "destroy", "destruction").
2. **Synonym**: One mention's word is a synonym of the other's word.
3. **Wide-reading**: One mention is a synonym of the wide reading of the other (defined below, under Quasi-identity:Scriptal). For example, in "the attack(E1) took place yesterday. The bombing(E2) killed four people", E1 and E2 are fully coreferent only when "bombing" is read in its wide sense that denotes the whole attack, not the narrow sense that denotes just the actual exploding of the bomb.
4. **Paraphrase**: One mention is a paraphrase of the other. Here some syntactic differences may occur. Some examples are active/passive transformation ("she gave him the book" / "he was given the book by her"), shifts of perspective that do not add or lose information ("he went to Boston" / "he came to Boston"), etc. No extra semantic information is provided in one mention or the other.
5. **Pronoun**: One mention refers deictically to the DE, as in ("the party" / "that event"), ("the election [went well]" / "it [went well]").

2.2 Quasi-identity

Mention1 is quasi- (partially) identical to mention2 iff they refer to the 'same' DE but one mention includes information that is not contained in the other, not counting information understood/inherited from the context. They are semantically not fully identical, though the core part of the two mentions is. One mention can replace the other, but some information will be changed, added, or lost. (This is the typical case between possible coreferent mentions within a document.)

We distinguish between two core types of partial identity: Membership and Subevent. The essential difference between the two is which aspects of the two events in question differ. Member-of obtains when we have two instances of the same event that differ in some particulars, such as time and location and [some] participants (agents, patients, etc). In contrast, Subevent obtains when we have different events that occur at more or less the same place and time with the same cast of participants.

Membership: Mention1 is a set of similar DEs (multiple instances of the same kind of event), like several birthday parties, and mention2 is one or more of them. More precisely, we say that an event B is a **member** of A if: (i) A is a set of multiple instances of the same type of event (and hence its mention usually pluralized); (ii) B's DE(s) is one or more (but not all) of them; (iii) either or both the time and the place of B's DE(s) and (some of) A's DEs are different. For example, in "I attended three parties(E1) last month. The first one(E2) was the best", E2 is a member of E1. The relation that links the single instance to the set is **member-of**.

Subevent: The DE of mention1 is a script (a stereotypical sequence of events, performed by an agent in pursuit of a given goal, such as eating at a restaurant, executing a bombing, running for election), and mention2 is one of the actions/events executed as part of that script (say, paying the waiter, or detonating the bomb, or making a campaign speech). More precisely, we say that an event B is a **subevent** of an event A if: (i) A is a complex sequence of activities, mostly performed by the same (or compatible) agent; (ii) B is one of these activities; and (iii) B occurs at the same time and place as A. Here A acts as a kind of collector event. Often, the whole script is named by the key event of the script (for example, in "he planned the explosion", the "explosion" signifies the whole script, including planning, planting the bomb, the detonation, etc.; but the actual detonation event itself can also be called "the explosion"). We call the interpretation of the mention that refers to the whole script its *wide reading*, and the interpretation that refers to just the key subevent the *narrow reading*. It is important not to confuse the two; a wide reading and a narrow reading of a word cannot corefer[3]. The relation that links the narrow reading DE to the wide one is **sub-to**.

Several aspects of the events in question provide key information to differentiate between members and subevents:

1. **Time**: When the time of occurrence of mention1 is temporally 'close enough' to the time of occurrence of mention2, then it is likely that one is a Subevent of the other. More precisely, we say that an event B is a **subevent** of event A if: (i) A and B are both events; (ii) the mentions of A and B both refer to the same overall DE; and (iii) the time of occurrence of B is contained in the time of occurrence of A. But if (i) and (ii) hold but not (iii), and A is a set of events (plural), then B is a member of A. (In (Humphreys et al., 1997), any variation in time automatically results in a decision of non-coreference.)

2. **Space/location**: The location of mention1 is spatially 'close enough' to the location of mention2. More precisely, we say that an event B is a **subevent** of event A if: (i) A and B are both events; (ii) the mentions of A and B both refer to the same overall DE; and (iii) the location of occurrence of B is contained in, or overlaps with, or abuts the location of occurrence of A. But if (i) and (ii) hold but not (iii), and A is a set of events (plural), then B is a member of A.

3. **Event participants**: Mention1 and mention2 refer to the same DE but differ in the overall cast of participants involved. In these cases, the **member** relation obtains, and can be differentiated into subtypes, since participants of events can differ in several ways. For example, if: (i) the mentions of events A and B refer to the same overall DE; and (ii) the participants (agents, patients, etc.) of mention2 are a subset of the participants of mention1, as in "the crowd demonstrated on the square. Susan and Mary were in it", then event B is a **participant-member** of event A. In another example, event B is a **participant-instance-member** of event A if: (i) the mentions of events A and B refer to the same overall DE; and (ii) one or more of the participants (agents, patients, etc.) of mention2 is/are an instance of the participants of mention1, as in "a firebrand addressed the crowd on the square. Joe spoke for an hour", where Joe is the firebrand.

There are other ways in which two mentions may refer to the same DE but differ from one another. Usually these differences are not semantic but reflect an orientation or perspective difference. For example, one mention may include the speaker's evaluation/opinion, while the other is neutral, as in "He sang the silly song. He embarrassed himself", or the spatial orientation of the speaker, as in "she went to New York" / "she came to New York". We treat these cases as fully coreferent.

Sometimes it is very difficult to know whether two mentions are bidirectionally implied, meaning that the two must corefer, or whether they are only quasi-identical (i.e., one entails the other but not vice versa). For example, in "he had a heart attack" / "he died", the two mentions are not identical because one can have a heart attack and not die from it. In contrast, "he had a fatal heart attack" / "he died from a heart attack" are identical. In "she was elected President" / "she took office as President", it is more difficult to decide. Does being elected automatically entail taking office? In some political systems it may, and in others it may not. When in doubt, we treat the case as only quasi-identical. Thus, comparing to examples from Full-Identity: Paraphrase, the following are only quasi-identical because of additional information: "she sold the book" / "she sold Peter the book"; "she sold Peter the book" / "Peter got [*not bought*] the book from her".

[3] For example, in "James perpetrated the shooting. He was arrested for the attack", "shooting" is used in its wide sense and here is coreferent with "attack", since it applies to a whole sequence of events. In contrast, "James perpetrated the shooting. He is the one who actually pulled the trigger", "shooting" is used in its narrow sense to mean just the single act. Typically, a word with two readings can corefer (i.e., be lexically or synonymically identical to) another in the same reading only.

Quasi-identity has been considered in coreference before in (Hasler et al., 2006) but not as extensively, and in (Recasens and Hovy, 2010a; 2011) but applied only to entities. When applied to events, the issue becomes more complex.

3 Two Problems

3.1 Domain and Reporting Events

As described above, inconsistent reporting occurs when a DE stated in reported text contains significant differences from the author's description of the same DE.

To handle such cases we have found it necessary to additionally identify communication events, which we call Reportings, during annotation because they provide a context in which a DE is stated. We identify two principal types of Reporting verbs: locutionary verbs "say", "report", "announce", etc.) and Speech Acts ("condemn", "promise", "support", "blame", etc.). Where the former verbs signal merely a telling, the latter verbs both say and thereby do something. For example in the following paragraph, "admitted" and "say" are communication events:

> Memon **admitted_R.7,in-sayR.3** his involvement in **activities_E.8,in-sayR.3** involving an explosives-laden van near the president's motorcade, police **said_R.3**". Sometimes the same event can participate inside two reporting events, as in "The LA Times **lauded_R.1** the **decision_E.2,in-sayR.1,in-sayR.3**, which the NY Times **lampooned_R.3**.

Though an added annotation burden, the link from a DE to a reporting event allows the analyst or learning system to discount apparent contradictory aspects of the DE and make more accurate identity decisions.

3.2 Unclear Semantics of Events

Sometimes it is difficult to determine the exact relationships between events since their semantics is unclear. In the following, is E.45 coreferent to E.44, or only partially? If so, how?

> Amnesty International has accused both sides of **violating_E.44** international humanitarian law by **targeting_E.45** civilian areas, and ...

We decided that E.44 is not fully coreferent with E.45, since violating is not the same as targeting. Also, E.45 is not a subevent of E.44 since "violating" is not a script with a well-defined series of steps, does not trigger "targeting", and does not occur before "targeting". Rather, targeting is a certain form or example of violation/violating. (It might be easier if the sentence were: "... of **violating** international humanitarian law **by targeting** civilian areas and the human rights group, **by killing** civilians, and **by....**". As such E.45 could be interpreted as a member of E.44, interpreting the latter as a series of violations.)

4 Annotation

To validate these ideas we have been annotating newspaper texts within the context of a large project on automated deep reading of text. This project combines Information Extraction, parsing, and various forms of inference to analyze a small number of texts and to then answer questions about them. The inability of current text analysis engines to handle event coreference has been a stumbling block in the project. By creating a corpus of texts annotated for coreference we are working to enable machine learning systems to learn which features are relevant for coreference and then ultimately to perform such coreference as well.

We are annotating two corpora:

1. The **Intelligence Community (IC) Corpus** contains texts in the Violent Events domain (bombings, killings, wars, etc.). Given the relative scarcity of the partial coreference subtypes, we annotated only instances of full coreference, Subevent, and Member relations. To handle Subevents one needs an unambiguous definition of the scripts in the domain. Fortunately this domain offers a manageable set of events (our event ontology comprises approximately 50 terms) with a subevent structure that is not overly complex but still realistic. We did not find the need to exceed three layers of scriptal granularity, as in *campaign* > {*bombing, attack*} > {*blast, kill, wound*}.

2. The **Biography (Bio) Corpus** contains texts describing the lives of famous people. Typically, these texts are written when the person dies or has some notable achievement. Given the complexities of description of artistic and other creative achievements, we restrict our corpus to achieve-

ments in politics, science, sports, and other more factual endeavors. More important than scriptal granularity in this domain is temporal sequencing.

We obtained and modified a version of the AnCoraPipe entity coreference annotation interface (Bertran et al., 2010) that was kindly given us by the AnCora team at the University of Barcelona. We implemented criteria and an automated method for automatically identifying domain and reporting events. We also created a tool to check and display the results of annotation, and technology to deliver various agreement scores.

Using different sets of annotators (from 3 to 6 people per text), we have completed a corpus of 100 texts in the IC domain and are in process of annotating the Bio corpus. Our various types of full and partial coreference and the associated annotation guidelines were developed and refined over the first third of these documents.

Table 1 shows statistics and inter-annotator agreement for the remaining 65 articles. The average number of domain and reporting events per article is 41.2. We use Fleiss's kappa since we have more than two annotators per article. The (rather low) score for member coreference is not really reliable given the small number of instances.

	Avg no per article	Agreement (Fleiss's kappa)
Full coreference relations	19.5	0.620
Member coreference relations	2.7	0.213
Subevent coreference relations	7.2	0.467

Table 1: Annotation statistics and agreement.

5 Validation and Use

To validate the conceptualization and definitions of full and partial identity relations, we report in (Araki et al., 2013) a study that determines correlations between the Member and Subevent relation instances and a variety of syntactic and lexico-semantic features. The utility of these features to support automated event coreference is reported in the same paper.

We are now developing a flexible recursive procedure that integrates coreference of events and of their pertinent participants (including locations and times). This procedure employs inference in addition to feature-based classification to compensate for the shortcomings of each method alone.

6 Relevant Past Work

The problem of identity has been addressed by scholars since antiquity. In the intensional approach (for example, De Saussure, 1896) a concept is defined as a set of attributes (differentiae), that serve to distinguish it from other concepts; two concepts are identical iff all their attributes and values are. In the extensional approach (Frege, 1982) a concept can be defined as the set of all instances of that concept; two concepts are identical when their two extensional sets are.

Given the impossibility of either approach to support practical work, AI scholars have devoted some attention to so-called Identity Criteria. Guarino (1999) outlines several 'dimensions' along which entities can remain identical or change under transformations; for example, a glass before and after it is crushed is identical with respect to its matter but not its shape; the ACL now and one hundred years hence is (probably) identical as an organization but not in its membership.

There has not been much theoretical work on semantic identity in the NLP community. But there has been a considerable amount of work on the problem of coreference. Focusing on entity coreference are (McCarthy and Lehnert, 1995; Culotta et al., 2007; Ng, 2007; Ng, 2009; Finkel and Manning, 2008; Ng, 2009). Focusing on event coreference are (Humphries et al., 1997; Chen and Zi, 2009; Bejan and Harabagiu, 2008; 2010).

Anaphora and bridging reference are discussed in (Poesio and Artstein, 2005; 2007). Relevant to events is the TIME-ML corpus (Mani and Pustejovsky, 2004; Pustejovsky et al., 2003), which provides a specification notation for events and temporal expressions.

Several corpora contain annotations for entity coreference, including the Prague Dependency Treebank (Kučová and Hajičová. 2004), the ACE corpus (Walker et al., 2006), and OntoNotes (Pradhan et al., 2007).

Most similar to our work is that of (Hasler et al., 2006). In that study, coreferential events and their arguments (also coreference between the arguments) were annotated for the terrorism/security domain, considering five event categories (attack, defend, injure, die, contact), and five event clusters (Bukavu bombing, Peru hostages, Tajikistan hostages, Israel suicide bombing and China-Taiwan hijacking). They also annotated information about the kind of coreferential link, such as *identity / synonymy / generalization / specialization / other*.

Our work takes further the ideas of (Hasler et al., 2006) and (Recasens et al., 2011) in elaborating the types of full and partial identity, as they are manifest in event coreference.

7 Conclusion

The problem of entity and event identity, and hence coreference, is challenging. We provide a definition of identity and two principal types of quasi-identity, with differentiation based on differences in location, time, and participants. We hope that these ideas help to clarify the problem and improve inter-annotator agreement.

Acknowledgments

Our grateful thanks goes to Prof. Antonia Martí and her team for their extensive work on the modifications of the AnCoraPipe annotation interface.

References

Araki, J., T, Mitamura, and E.H. Hovy. 2013. Identity and Quasi-Identity Relations for Event Coreference. Unpublished manuscript.

Bejan, C.A. and S. Harabagiu. 2008. A Linguistic Resource for Discovering Event Structures and Resolving Event Coreference. *Proceedings of the 6th International Conference on Language Resources and Evaluation (LREC 08).*

Bejan, C.A. and S. Harabagiu. 2010. Unsupervised Event Coreference Resolution with Rich Linguistic Features. *Proceedings of the 48th conference of the Association for Computational Linguistics (ACL 10).*

Bertran, M., O. Borrega, M.A. Martí, and M. Taulé, 2010. AnCoraPipe: A New Tool for Corpora Annotation. Working paper 1: TEXT-MESS 2.0 (Text-Knowledge 2.0). Available at http://clic.ub.edu/files/AnCoraPipe_0.pdf

Chen, Z. and H. Ji. 2009. Graph-based Event Coreference Resolution. *Proceedings of the ACL-IJCNLP 09 workshop on TextGraphs-4: Graph-based Methods for Natural Language Processing.*

Culotta, A., M. Wick, and A. McCallum. 2007. First-order probabilistic models for coreference resolution. *Proceedings of the HLT/NAACL conference.*

De Saussure, F. 1896. *Course in General Linguistics.* Open Court Classics.

Finkel, J.R. and C.D. Manning. 2008. Enforcing transitivity in coreference resolution. *Proceedings of the ACL-HLT conference,* pp. 45–48.

Florian, R., J F Pitrelli, S Roukos, I Zitouni. 2010. Improving Mention Detection Robustness to Noisy Input. *Proceedings of the Conference on Empirical Methods in Natural Language Processing (EMNLP).*

Frege, G. 1892. On Sense and Reference. Reprinted in P. Geach and M. Black (eds.) *Translations from the Philosophical Writings of Gottlob Frege.* Oxford: Blackwell, 1960.

Guarino, N. 1999. The Role of Identity Conditions in Ontology Design. In C. Freksa and D.M. Mark (eds.), *Spatial Information Theory: Cognitive and Computational Foundations of Geographic Information Science. Proceedings of International Conference COSIT '99.* Springer Verlag.

Hasler, L., C. Orasan, and K. Naumann. 2006. NPs for Events: Experiments in Coreference Annotation. *Proceedings of the 5th International Conference on Language Resources and Evaluation (LREC-06)*, pp. 1167–1172.

Hasler, L. and C. Orasan. 2009. Do Coreferential Arguments make Event Mentions Coreferential? *Proceedings of the 7th Discourse Anaphora and Anaphor Resolution Colloquium (DAARC 09)*, pp 151–163.

Humphreys, K., R. Gaizauskas and S. Azzam. 1997. Event Coreference for Information Extraction. *Proceedings of the ACL conference Workshop on Operational Factors in Practical, Robust Anaphora Resolution for Unrestricted Texts (ANARESOLUTION 97).*

Kučová, L. and E. Hajičová. 2004. Coreferential relations in the Prague Dependency Treebank. *Proceedings of the DAARC workshop*, pp. 97–102.

Mani, I. and J. Pustejovsky. 2004. Temporal Discourse Models for Narrative Structure. *Proceedings of the ACL 2004 Workshop on Discourse Annotation.*

McCarthy, J.F. and W. Lehnert. 1995. Using Decision trees for Coreference Resolution. *Proceedings of the IJCAI conference.*

Mill, J.S. 1872. *A System of Logic,* definitive 8th edition. 1949 reprint, London: Longmans, Green and Company.

Ng, V. 2007. Shallow Semantics for Coreference Resolution. *Proceedings of the IJCAI conference.*

Ng, V. 2009. Graph-cut-based Anaphoricity Determination for Coreference Resolution. *Proceedings of the NAACL-HLT conference*, pp. 575–583.

Poesio, M. and R. Artstein. 2005. The reliability of anaphoric annotation, reconsidered: Taking ambiguity into account. *Proceedings of the ACL Workshop on Frontiers in Corpus Annotation II.*

Poesio, M. and R. Artstein. 2008. Anaphoric annotation in the ARRAU corpus. *Proceedings of the LREC conference.*

Pradhan, S., E.H. Hovy, M. Marcus, M. Palmer, L. Ramshaw, and R. Weischedel 2007. OntoNotes: A Unified Relational Semantic Representation. *International Journal of Semantic Computing* 1(4), pp. 405–420.

Pustejovsky, J., J. Castaño, R. Ingria, R. Saurí, R. Gaizauskas, A. Setzer and G. Katz. 2003. TimeML: Robust Specification of Event and Temporal Expressions in Text. *Proceedings of IWCS-5, Fifth International Workshop on Computational Semantics.*

Recasens, M. and E.H. Hovy. 2010a. Coreference Resolution across Corpora: Languages, Coding Schemes, and Preprocessing Information. *Proceedings of the Association of Computational Linguistics conference (ACL 10).*

Recasens, M. and E.H. Hovy. 2010b. BLANC: Implementing the Rand Index for Coreference Evaluation. *Journal of Natural Language Engineering* 16(5).

Recasens, M., E.H. Hovy, and M.A. Martí. 2011. Identity, Non-identity, and Near-identity: Addressing the Complexity of Coreference. *Lingua.*

Taulé, M., M.A. Martí. and M. Recasens. 2008. AnCora: Multilevel Annotated Corpora for Catalan and Spanish. *Proceedings of the LREC 08 conference*, pp. 96–101.

Walker, C., S. Strassel, J. Medero 2006. The ACE 2005 multilingual training corpus. Linguistic Data Consortium, University of Pennsylvania, Philadelphia.

Event representation across genre

Lidia Pivovarova, Silja Huttunen and Roman Yangarber

University of Helsinki
Finland

Abstract

This paper describes an approach for investigating the representation of events and their distribution in a corpus. We collect and analyze statistics about subject-verb-object triplets and their content, which helps us compare corpora belonging to the same domain but to different genre/text type. We argue that event structure is strongly related to the genre of the corpus, and propose statistical properties that are able to capture these genre differences. The results obtained can be used for the improvement of Information Extraction.

1 Introduction

The focus of this paper is collecting data about certain characteristics of events found in text, in order to improve the performance of an Information Extraction (IE) system. IE is a technology used for locating and extracting specific pieces of information—or "facts"—from unstructured natural-language text, by transforming the facts into abstract, structured objects, called *events*.

In IE we assume that events represent real-world facts and the main objective is to extract them from plain text; the nature of the events themselves rarely receives in-depth attention in current research.

Events may have various relationships to real-world facts, and different sources may have contradictory views on the facts, (Saurí and Pustejovsky, 2012). Similarly to many other linguistic units, an event is a combination of meaning and form; the structure and content of an event is influenced by both the structure of the corresponding real-world fact and by the properties of the surrounding text.

We use the notion of *scenario* to denote a set of structured events of interest in a real-world domain: e.g., the MUC Management Succession scenario, (Grishman and Sundheim, 1996), within the broader Business domain.

The representation and the structure of events in text depends on the scenario. For example, Huttunen et al. (2002a; Huttunen et al. (2002b) points out that "classic" MUC scenarios, such as Management Succession or Terrorist Attacks, describe events that occur in a specific point in time, whereas other scenarios like Natural Disaster or Disease Outbreak describe processes that are spread out across time and space. As a consequence, events in the latter, "nature"-related scenarios are more complex, may have a hierarchical structure, and may overlap with each other in text. Linguistic cues that have been proposed in Huttunen et al. (2002a) to identify the overlapping or partial events include specific lexical items, locative and temporal expressions, and usage of ellipsis and anaphora.

Grishman (2012) has emphasized that for fully unsupervised event extraction, extensive linguistic analysis is essential; such analysis should be able to capture "modifiers on entities, including quantity and measure phrases and locatives; modifiers on predicates, including negation, aspect, quantity, and temporal information; and higher-order predicates, including sequence and causal relations and verbs of belief and reporting." It is clear that such sophisticated linguistic analysis increases the importance of text style and genre for Information Extraction.

The idea of statistical comparison between text types goes back at least as far as (Biber, 1991). It was subsequently used in a number of papers on automatic text categorization (Kessler et al., 1997; Stamatatos et al., 2000; Petrenz and Webber, 2011).

Szarvas et al. (2012) studied the linguistic cues indicating uncertainty of events in three genres: news, scientific papers and Wikipedia articles. They demonstrate significant differences in lexical usage across the genres; for example, such words as *fear* or *worry* may appear relatively often in news and Wikipedia, but almost never in scientific text. They also investigate differences in syntactic cues: for example, the relation between a proposition and a real-word fact is more likely to be expressed in the passive voice in scientific papers (*it is expected*), whereas in news the same words are more likely appear in the active.

Because events are not only representations of facts but also linguistic units, an investigation of events should take into account the particular language, genre, scenario and medium of the text—i.e., events should be studied in the context of a *particular corpus*. Hence, the next question is how corpus-driven study of events should be organized in practice, or, more concretely, what particular statistics are needed to capture the scenario-specific characteristics of event representation in a particular corpus, and what kind of markup is necessary to solve this task. We believe that answers to these questions will likely depend on the ultimate goals of event detection. We investigate IE in the business domain—thus, we believe that preliminary study of the corpus should use exactly the same depth of linguistic analysis as would be later utilized by the IE system.

2 Problem Statement

2.1 Events in the Business domain

We investigate event structure in the context of PULS,[1] an IE System, that discovers, aggregates, verifies and visualizes events in various scenarios. This paper focuses on the Business domain, in which scenarios include investments, contracts, layoffs and other business-related events, which are collected in a database to be used for decision support. In the Business domain, PULS currently handles two types of documents: news reports and short summaries written by professional business analysts. Thus, events extracted from both corpora relate to approximately the same real-world facts.

[1]More information is available at: http://puls.cs.helsinki.fi

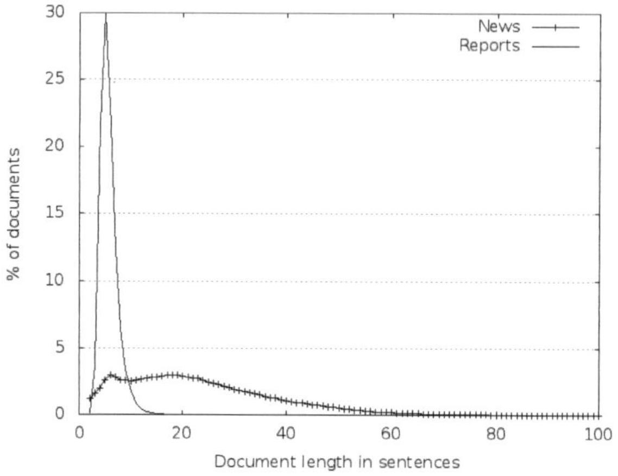

Figure 1: Distributions of document length in the news and business analysts' reports corpora

Both corpora are in English (though some of the analysts' reports are based on news articles written in other languages). We collected a corpus of reports containing 740 thousand documents over three years 2010-2012, and a news corpus containing 240 thousand documents over the same period.

The two corpora demonstrate significant linguistic differences. First, the documents have different length: the average length of an analyst reports is 5.5 sentences including the title, and 80% of the documents have length between 4 and 7 sentences, (see Figure 1). News articles are on average 19 sentences long—and much more varied in length.

The topical structure is also quite different for the two corpora. Each analyst report is most typically dedicated to a particular single real-world event. Also, the reports tend to have a standardized, formulaic structure. The analysts who generate these reports tend to follow a specific, strict style and structure over time.

By contrast, documents in the news corpus are much more heterogeneous. These texts can follow a wide variety of different styles—short messages, surveys, interviews, etc. News documents can focus not only strictly on business events but on related topics as well. For example, political events have complex interaction with and impact on business activity, and therefore political news frequently appear in business news feeds.

PULS aims to use the same processing chain for various types of input documents. One key goal of the current work is to investigate whether different IE processing approaches are needed for documents belonging to different text types, as exemplified by analyst reports vs. articles from news feeds.

To summarize, the goals of the present work are:

- investigate how text genre influences event representation;
- find formal markers able to capture and measure the differences in corpus style/genre;
- propose a methodology for adaptating an IE system to a different text genre.

2.2 System Description

In this section we describe how the IE system is used in a "pattern-mining mode," to address the aforementioned problems.

PULS is a pipeline of components, including: a shallow parser/chunker; domain ontologies and lexicons; low-level patterns for capturing domain-specific entities and other semantic units, such as dates and currency expressions; higher-level patterns for capturing domain-specific relations and events; inference rules, which combine fragments of an event that may be scattered in text—that a pattern may not have picked up in the immediate context (e.g., the date of the event); reference resolution for merging co-referring entities and events.

The ontology and the lexicon for the Business domain encode the taxonomic relations and support merging of synonyms: e.g., the ontology stores the information that *cellphone* and *mobile phone* are synonymous, and that a super-concept for both is PRODUCT.

Low-level patterns are used to extract entities from text, such as company names, dates, and locations. On a slightly higher level, there are patterns that match contexts such as *range (collection, line, etc.) of X* and assign them the type of *X*. For instance, the phrase *a collection of watches* would be assigned semantic type *watch*, etc. The top-level patterns in all IE scenarios are responsible for finding the target events in text.

In the pattern-mining mode we use the general pattern SUBJECT–VERB–OBJECT, where the components may have any semantic type and are constrained only by their *deep* syntactic function—the system attempts to normalize many syntactic variants of the basic, active form: including passive clauses, relative clauses, etc.[2]

The idea of using very simple, local patterns for obtaining information from large corpora in the context of event extraction is similar to work reported previously, e.g., the bootstrapping approaches in (Thelen and Riloff, 2002; Yangarber et al., 2000; Riloff and Shepherd, 1997). Here, we do not use iterative learning, and focus instead on collecting and analyzing interesting statistics from a large number of S-V-O patterns. We collected all such "generalized" S-V-O triplets from the corpus and stored them in a database. In addition to the noun groups, we save the head nouns and their semantic classes. This makes it easy to use simple SQL queries to count instances of a particular pattern, e.g., all objects of a particular verb, or all actions that can be applied to an object of semantic class "PRODUCT." For each triplet the database stores a pointer the original sentence, making it possible to analyze specific examples in their context.

In the next two sections we present the statistics that we collected using the pattern-mining mode. This information reflects significant differences among the corpora genres and can be used to *measure* variety of genre. We believe that in the future such data analysis will support the adaptation of PULS to new text genres.

3 Statistical Properties of the Corpora

3.1 Personal pronouns

Pronouns play a key role in anaphoric relations; the more pronouns are present in the corpus, the more crucial anaphora resolution becomes. Analysis of relationships between frequencies of personal pronouns in text and the genre of the text is not new; it has been observed and studied extensively, going

[2]By normalization of syntactic variants we mean, for instance, that clauses like *"Nokia releases a new cellphone"* (active), *"a new cellphone is released by Nokia"* (passive), *"a new cellphone, released by Nokia,..."* (relative), etc., are all reduced to the same S-V-O form.

Pronoun	Reports		News	
	Object	*Subject*	*Object*	*Subject*
I/me	0.003	0.007	0.2	1.0
we/us	0.001	0.001	0.4	1.7
you	0.002	0.003	0.3	0.8
he/him	0.05	0.4	0.6	2.2
she/her	0.007	0.05	0.1	0.5
they/them	0.3	0.6	0.8	1.3
it	1.1	2.6	1.5	2.3
Total	**1.5**	**3.6**	**4.0**	**9.8**

Table 1: Personal pronouns appearing in the subject or object position in the corpora. The numerical values are proportions of the total number of verbs.

back as far as, e.g., (Karlgren and Cutting, 1994). The analysis of pronoun distribution in our corpora is presented in Table 1, which shows the proportions of personal pronouns, as they appear in subject or object position with verbs in the collected triples. The numbers are relative to the count of all verb tokens in the corpus, i.e., the total number of the S–V–O triplets extracted from the corpus. The total number of triplets is approximately 5.7M in the report corpus and 11M in the news corpus.

It can be seen from Table 1 that personal pronouns are much more rare in the report corpus than in the news corpus. Only 1.5% of verbs in the reports corpus have a pronoun as an object, and 3.6% as a subject. By contrast, in the news corpus 4% of verbs have a personal pronoun as an object, and 9.8% as a subject. This corresponds to the observation in (Szarvas et al., 2012), that "impersonal constructions are hardly used in news media."

It is interesting to note the distribution of the particular pronouns in the two corpora. Table 1 shows that *it* is the most frequent pronoun, *they* and *he* are less frequent; the remaining pronouns are much less frequent in the report corpus, whereas in the news the remaining personal pronouns have a much more even distribution. This clearly reflects a more relaxed style of the news that may use rhetorical devices more freely, including citing direct speech and use a direct addressing the reader (*you*). It is also interesting to note that in the third-person singular, the feminine pronoun is starkly more rare in both corpora than the masculine, but roughly twice more rare among the analyst reports.

	Reports		News	
	Subject	*Object*	*Subject*	*Object*
All	21.8	6.6	14.6	6.5
Business	27.1	8.1	20.1	9.5

Table 2: Distribution of proper names as subjects and objects, as a proportion the total number of all verbs (top row) vs. *business-related* verbs (bottom row).

3.2 Proper Names

Proper names play a crucial role in co-reference resolution, by designating anaphoric relations in text, similarly to pronouns. In the Business domain, e.g., a common noun phrase (NP) may co-refer with a proper name, as "the company" may refer to the name of a particular firm. A correctly extracted event can be much less useful for the end-user if it does not contain the specific name of the company involved in the event.

A verbs is often the key element of a pattern that indicates to the IE system the presence of an event of interest in the text. When the subject or object of the verb is a common NP, the corresponding proper name must be found in the surrounding context, using reference resolution or domain-specific inference rules. Since reference resolution is itself a phase that contributes some amount of error to the overall IE process, it is natural to expect that if proper-name subjects and objects are more frequent in the corpus, then the analysis can be more precise, since all necessary information can be extracted by pattern without the need for additional extra inference. Huttunen et al. (2012) suggests that the compactness of the event representation may be used as one of the discourse cues that determine the event relevance.

Table 2 shows the percentage of proper name objects and subjects for the two corpora. Proper-name objects have comparable frequency in both corpora, though proper-name subjects appear much more frequently in analyst reports than in news. Furthermore, for the *business verbs*, introduced below in section 4.1—i.e., the specific set of verbs that are used in event patterns in the Business scenarios—as seen in the second row of the table—proper-name objects and subjects are more frequent still. This suggests that business events *tend* to mention proper names.

	Percentage of business verbs		
Corpus	*Total*	*Title*	*1st sentence*
Reports	49.5	7.6	13.8
News	31.8	0.6	1.1

Table 3: Business verbs in analyst reports and news corpora, as a proportion of the total number of verbs.

4 Business Verbs

4.1 Distribution of Business verbs

The set of *business-related verbs* is an important part of the system's domain-specific lexicon for the Business domain. These verbs are quite diverse: some are strongly associated with the Business domain, e.g., *invest*; some are more general, e.g., *pay, make*; many are ambiguous, e.g., *launch, fire*. Inside analyst reports these verbs always function as markers of certain business events or relations. The verbs are the key elements of the top-level patterns and it is especially crucial to investigate their usage in the corpora to understand how the pattern base should be fine-tune for the task.

Since the majority of these verbs fall in the ambiguous category, none of these verbs can by themselves serve a sufficient indicator of the document's topic. Even the more clear-cut business verbs, such as *invest*, can be used metaphorically in the non-business context. However, their *distribution* in the particular document and in the corpus as a whole can reflect the genre specificity of the corpus.

Table 3 shows the overall proportion of the business verbs, and their proportion in titles and in the first sentence of a documents. It suggests that almost 50% of the verbs in the report corpus are "business" verbs, and almost half of them are concentrated in the beginning of a document. By contrast, the fraction of business verbs in the news corpus is less than one third and they are more scattered through the text. This fact is illustrated by the plot in Figure 2.

The first sentence is often the most informative part of text, since it introduces the topic of the document to the reader and the writer must do his/her best to attract the reader's attention. It was shown in (Huttunen et al., 2012) that 65% of highly-relevant events in the domain of medical epidemics appear in the title or in the first two sentences of a news article; Lin and Hovy (1997) demonstrated that

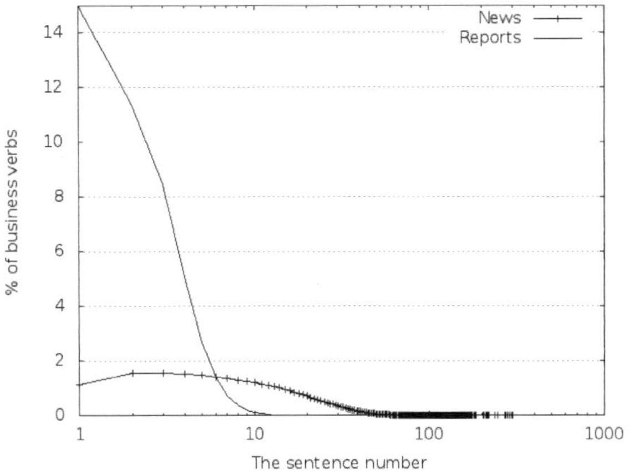

Figure 2: Percentage of business verbs in the text; sentence 0 refers to the title of the document. The fraction of verbs is presented as a percent of all verb instances in the corpus. Logarithmic scale is used for the x axis.

about 50% of topical keywords are concentrated in the titles. We have noticed that some documents in the news corpus have relevance to the business scenario, although relevant events still can be extracted from the second or third paragraphs of the text, mentioned incidentally. By contrast, each analyst report is devoted to a specific business event, and these events are frequently mentioned as early as in the title.

4.2 Case study: is "launch" a business verb?

A set of verbs such as *launch, introduce, release, present*,[3] etc., are used in the Business scenarios to extract events about bringing new products to market. In the domain ontology they are grouped under a concept called *LAUNCH-PRODUCT*. An example of a pattern that uses this concept is following:

```
np(COMPANY) vg(LAUNCH-PRODUCT)
    np(ANYTHING)
```

This pattern matches when a NP designating a company is followed by a verb from the ontology, followed by any other NP. This pattern matches, for example, such sentence as: *The Real Juice Company has launched Pomegranate Blueberry flavour to its line of 100% juices.* However, this pattern also over-generates by matching sentences such as, e.g.: *Cen-*

[3]Note, the S-V-O triplet extraction also handles phrasal verbs, such as *roll out*, correctly, i.e., identifies them as a single linguistic unit, and treats them the same as single-word verbs.

tral bank unveils effort to manage household debt. Even among analyst reports, approximately 14% of the NEW-PRODUCT events found by the system are false positives. It is not feasible to collect a list of all possible products to restrict the semantic type of the object of the verb, since new, unpredictable types of products can appear on the market every day. It seemed more feasible to try to discover all *non-products* that can appear in the object slot, due to the ambiguity of the verbs in patterns—a kind of a black-list. We introduce an ontology concept NON-PRODUCT that groups nouns that can be matched by the LAUNCH verbs but are in fact not products, e.g., *budget, effort, plan, report, study*. The ontology supports multiple inheritance, so any of these words can be attached to other parents as well, if necessary.

If the <PRODUCT> slot in of event is filled by one of the black-listed concepts, the event is also black-listed, and not visible to the end-user. They are used as discourse features by learning algorithms that predict the relevance of other events from the same documents (Huttunen et al., 2012).

The NON-PRODUCT class is populated in an ad-hoc manner over time. The content of such a list depends on the particular corpus; the more diverse the topical and stylistic structure of the corpus, the more time-consuming and the less tractable such development becomes. Thus, an important task is to adjust the patterns and the class of NON-PRODUCT nouns to work for the news corpus, and to develop a feasible methodology to address the false-positive problem. We next show how we can use the pattern-mining mode to address these problems.

We extract all instances of the LAUNCH-PRODUCT verbs appearing in the corpora from the S–V–O database. In total 27.5% of all verb instances in reports corpus are verbs from this semantic class, in comparison to 0.7% in the news corpus. The number of distinct objects are approximately the same in both corpora: 3520 for reports and 3062 for news, see Table 4. In total 247 different objects from the report corpus attached to the semantic class PRODUCT in PULS ontology, and 158 objects have this semantic class in the news corpus.

For 21% of *launch* verbs in the report corpus, and 34% in the news corpus, the system is not able to extract the objects, which may be a consequence of the more diverse and varied language of news. Recall,

Corpus	LAUNCH-PRODUCT	distinct objects	PRODUCT objects
Reports	204193	3520	247
News	77463	3062	158

Table 4: Distributions of LAUNCH-PRODUCT verbs in the corpora

that the system extracts a *deep-structure* verbal arguments, i.e., for a sentence like *"A new cell-phone has been launched by company XYZ"* it identifies *cell-phone* as the (deep) object, and the agent *company XYZ* as the (deep) subject.

It is interesting to examine the particular sets of words that can appear in the object position. We collected the 50 most frequent objects of the LAUNCH-PRODUCT verbs for each corpus; they are shown in Table 5 ranked by frequency (we show the top 30 objects to save space). The table shows the semantic class according to our ontology.

Of the 50 most frequent objects, 24 belong to the semantic class PRODUCT in the report corpus, while only 8 objects do in the general news corpus. By contrast, 20 objects belong to the NON-PRODUCT class in the news corpus and only 9 objects in reports. Moreover, 8 objects in the news corpus are not found in the ontology at all, in comparison to only one such case from the report corpus.

Some object classes may mean that the event is still relevant for the business domain, though it does not belong to the NEW-PRODUCT scenario. For example, when object is an advertising campaign the event is likely to belong to the MARKETING scenario, when the object is a facility (*factory, outlet, etc.*) it is likely INVESTMENT. Inference rules may detect such dependencies and adjust the scenario of these events in the Business domain.

The inference rules are supported by the same domain ontology, but can test domain- and scenario-specific conditions explicitly, and thus can be more accurate than the generic reference resolution mechanism. However, this also means that inference rules are more sensitive to the corpus genre and may not easily transfer from one corpus to another.

In some cases an object type cannot be interpreted as belonging to any reasonable event type, e.g., if it is an ORGANIZATION or PERSON. Such cases may arise due to unusual syntax in the sentence that

Rank	Reports			News		
	Object	**Freq**	**Class**	**Object**	**Freq**	**Class**
1	*Proper Name unspecified*	19987		*Proper Name unspecified*	5971	
2	product	7331	PROD	report	1078	NON
3	service	6510	PROD	result	851	NON
4	campaign	3537	CAMP	plan	805	NON
5	project	2870	PROD	product	792	PROD
6	range	2536	COLL	service	648	PROD
7	plan	2524	NON	it	618	PRON
8	organization	2450	ORG	data	552	
9	system	2166	FAC	campaign	510	CAMP
10	line	1938	COLL	organization	495	ORG
11	model	1920	PROD	statement	467	NON
12	application	1345	PROD	*Proper Name person*	449	PER
13	website	1321	PROD	program	439	
14	flight	1315	PROD	*Proper Name company*	432	ORG
15	*Proper Name company*	1232	ORG	information	411	NON
16	brand	1200	COLL	detail	398	NON
17	offer	1187	NON	investigation	380	NON
18	production	1112	NON	website	373	PROD
19	programme	998	NON	measure	368	NON
20	store	993	PROD	they	363	PRON
21	*currency*	958	CUR	he	358	PRON
22	route	954	PROD	device	352	PROD
23	drink	891	PROD	system	340	FAC
24	solution	883	NON	smartphone	337	PROD
25	smartphone	852	PROD	attack	335	
26	fragrance	824	PROD	figure	318	NON
27	card	802	PROD	opportunity	295	INV
28	fund	801	PROD	fund	290	NON
29	scheme	773	NON	*currency*	287	CUR
30	facility	756	FAC	model	286	COLL

Table 5: The most frequent objects of LAUNCH verbs. Class labels: PROD: product, NON: non-product (blacklisted), CAMP: advertising campaign, INV: investment. Domain independent labels: COLL: collective; PRON: pronoun, FAC: facility, ORG: organization, PER: person, CUR: currency,

confuses the shallow parser.

In summary, the results obtained from the S-V-O pattern-mining can be used to improve the performance of IE. First, the most frequent subjects and objects for the business verbs can be added to the ontology; second, inference rules and patterns are adjusted to handle the new concepts and words.

It is very interesting to investigate—and we plan to pursue this in the future—how this can be done fully automatically; the problem is challenging since the semantic classes for these news concepts depend on the domain and task; for example, some objects are of type PRODUCT (e.g., "video"), and others are of type NON-PRODUCT (e.g., "attack", "report", etc.). Certain words can be ambiguous even within a limited domain: e.g., *player* may designate a COMPANY ("a major player on the market"), a PRODUCT (DVD-player, CD-player, etc.), or a person (tennis player, football player, etc.); the last meaning is relevant for the Business domain since sports personalities participate in promotion campaigns, and can launch their own brands. Automating the construction of the knowledge bases is a challenging task.

In practice, we found that the semi-automated approach and the pattern-mining tool can be helpful for analyzing genre-specific event patterns; it provides the advantages of a corpus-based study.

5 Conclusion

We have described an approach for collecting useful statistics about event representation and distribution of event arguments in corpora. The approach was easily implemented using pattern-based extraction of S-V-O triplets with PULS; it can be equally efficiently implemented on top of a syntactic parser, or a shallow parser of reasonable quality. An ontology and lexicons are necessary to perform domain-specific analysis. We have discussed how the results of such analysis can be exploited for fine-tuning of a practical IE scenario.

The pattern-mining process collects *deep-structure* S–V–O triplets from the corpus—which are "potential" events. The triplets are stored in a database, to facilitate searching and grouping by words or by semantic class appearing as the arguments of the triplets. This helps us quickly find all realizations of a particular pattern—for example, all semantic classes that appear in the corpus as objects of verbs that have semantic class LAUNCH-PRODUCT. The subsequent analysis of the frequency lists can help improve the performance of the IE system by suggesting refinements to the ontology and the lexicon, as well as patterns and inference rules appropriate for the particular genre of the corpus.

Our current work includes the adaptation of the IE system developed for the analyst reports to the general news corpus devoted to the same topics. We also plan to develop a hybrid methodology, to combine the presented corpus-driven analysis with open-domain techniques for pattern acquisition, (Chambers and Jurafsky, 2011; Huang and Riloff, 2012).

The approach outlined here for analyzing the distributions of features in documents is useful for studying events within the context of a corpus. It demonstrates that event structure depends on the text genre, and that genre differences can be easily captured and measured. By analyzing document statistics and the output of the pattern-mining, we can demonstrate significant differences between the genres of analyst reports and general news, such as: sentence length, distribution of the domain vocabulary in the text, selectional preference in domain-specific verbs, word co-occurrences, usage of pronouns and proper names.

The pattern mining collects other statistical features, beyond those that have been discussed in detail above. For example, it showed that active voice is used in 95% of the cases in the news corpus in comparison to 88% in the analyst report corpus. It is also possible to count and compare the usage of other grammatical cues, such as verb tense, modality, etc. Thus, we should investigate not only lexical and semantic cues, but also broader syntactic preferences and selectional constrains in the corpora.

In further research we plan to study how the formal representation of the genre differences can be used in practice, that is, for obtaining directly measurable improvements in the quality of event extraction. Taking into account the particular genre of the corpora from which documents are drawn will also have implications for the work on performance improvements via cross-document merging and inference, (Ji and Grishman, 2008; Yangarber, 2006).

The frequency-based analysis described in Section 4.2 seems to be effective. Sharpening the results of the analysis as well as putting it to use in practical IE applications will be the subject of further study.

Acknowledgements

We wish to thank Matthew Pierce and Peter von Etter for their help in implementation of the pattern mining more described in this paper. The work was supported in part by the ALGODAN: Algorithmic Data Analysis Centre of Excellence of the Academy of Finland.

References

Douglas Biber. 1991. *Variation across speech and writing*. Cambridge University Press.

Nathanael Chambers and Dan Jurafsky. 2011. Template-based information extraction without the templates. In *Proceedings of ACL-HLT*, pages 976–986.

Ralph Grishman and Beth Sundheim. 1996. Message understanding conference-6: A brief history. In *Proceedings of COLING*, volume 96, pages 466–471.

Ralph Grishman. 2012. Structural linguistics and unsupervised information extraction. *Automatic Knowledge Base Construction and Web-scale Knowledge Extraction (AKBC-WEKEX 2012)*, pages 57–61.

Ruihong Huang and Ellen Riloff. 2012. Bootstrapped training of event extraction classifiers. *EACL 2012*, pages 286–295.

Silja Huttunen, Roman Yangarber, and Ralph Grishman. 2002a. Complexity of event structure in IE scenarios. In *Proceedings of the 19th International Conference on Computational Linguistics (COLING 2002)*, Taipei, August.

Silja Huttunen, Roman Yangarber, and Ralph Grishman. 2002b. Diversity of scenarios in information extraction. In *Proceedings of the Third International Conference on Language Resources and Evaluation (LREC 2002)*, Las Palmas de Gran Canaria, Spain, May.

Silja Huttunen, Arto Vihavainen, Mian Du, and Roman Yangarber. 2012. Predicting relevance of event extraction for the end user. In T. Poibeau et al., editor, *Multi-source, Multilingual Information Extraction and Summarization*, pages 163–177. Springer-Verlag, Berlin.

Heng Ji and Ralph Grishman. 2008. Refining event extraction through cross-document inference. In *Proceedings of ACL-2008: HLT*, pages 254–262, June.

Jussi Karlgren and Douglas Cutting. 1994. Recognizing text genres with simple metrics using discriminant analysis. In *Proceedings of the 15th Conference on Computational Linguistics*, pages 1071–1075, Kyoto, Japan, August.

Brett Kessler, Geoffrey Numberg, and Hinrich Schütze. 1997. Automatic detection of text genre. In *Proceedings of the 35th Annual Meeting of the Association for Computational Linguistics and Eighth Conference of the European Chapter of the Association for Computational Linguistics*, pages 32–38. Association for Computational Linguistics.

Chin-Yew Lin and Eduard Hovy. 1997. Identifying topics by position. In *Proceedings of the fifth conference on Applied natural language processing*, pages 283–290. Association for Computational Linguistics.

Philipp Petrenz and Bonnie Webber. 2011. Stable classification of text genres. *Computational Linguistics*, 37(2):385–393.

Ellen Riloff and Jessica Shepherd. 1997. A corpus-based approach for building semantic lexicons. In *Proceedings of the Second Conference on Empirical Methods in Natural Language Processing*, pages 117–124. Association for Computational Linguistics, Somerset, New Jersey.

Roser Saurí and James Pustejovsky. 2012. Are you sure that this happened? Assessing the factuality degree of events in text. *Computational Linguistics*, 38(2):261–299.

Efstathios Stamatatos, Nikos Fakotakis, and George Kokkinakis. 2000. Text genre detection using common word frequencies. In *Proceedings of the 18th conference on Computational linguistics - Volume 2*, COLING '00, pages 808–814, Stroudsburg, PA, USA. Association for Computational Linguistics.

György Szarvas, Veronika Vincze, Richárd Farkas, György Móra, and Iryna Gurevych. 2012. Cross-genre and cross-domain detection of semantic uncertainty. *Computational Linguistics*, 38(2):335–367.

Mark Thelen and Ellen Riloff. 2002. A bootstrapping method for learning semantic lexicons using extraction pattern contexts. In *Proceedings of the 2002 Conference on Empirical Methods in Natural Language Processing (EMNLP 2002)*.

Roman Yangarber, Ralph Grishman, Pasi Tapanainen, and Silja Huttunen. 2000. Automatic acquisition of domain knowledge for information extraction. In *Proceedings of the 18th International Conference on Computational Linguistics (COLING 2000)*, Saarbrücken, Germany, August.

Roman Yangarber. 2006. Verification of facts across document boundaries. In *Proceedings of the International Workshop on Intelligent Information Access (IIIA-2006)*, Helsinki, Finland, August.

A Semantic Tool for Historical Events

Ryan Shaw
School of Information and Library Science
University of North Carolina at Chapel Hill
ryanshaw@unc.edu

Abstract

I present a set of functional requirements for a speculative tool informing users about events in historical discourse, in order to demonstrate what these requirements imply about how we should define and represent historical events. The functions include individuation, selection, and contextualization of events. I conclude that a tool providing these functions would need events to be defined and represented as features of discourses about the world rather than objectively existing things in the world.

1 Introduction

Most work in NLP on detecting and representing events tacitly adopts a theory of events that can be traced to Donald Davidson. The advantage of this theory is that it promises to provide a solid foundation for consensus on how to define and individuate events. But that consensus will be useful for specific domains of application only to the extent that it aligns with the way events are conceptualized in those domains. In domains where events serve conceptual functions that differ significantly from the ones assumed by that consensus, it may actually retard the development of practical tools.

History is one such domain. Automatic detection of events and their coreference relations would be a powerful tool for working with and learning from collections of historical texts. But events as conceptualized by historians differ in significant ways from events as theorized by analytic philosophers. Rather than attempting to formulate an alternative theory, I instead present a set of high-level requirements for a speculative tool that would benefit from automatic detection of historical events and their coreference relations. That is, rather than looking for a foundational theory to guide the definition and representation of events, I start by envisioning a useful tool and then try to determine how events would need to be defined and represented in order to create that tool.

The speculative vision I present is a semantic tool for informing users about events in historical discourse. A *semantic tool* is any instrument that can inform its users about concepts of interest in some domain, various names or terms associated with those concepts, and relationships among concepts (Hjørland, 2007). Examples include dictionaries, gazetteers, taxonomies, thesauri, and ontologies.

I have purposefully chosen to present a highly speculative, "blue sky" vision for two reasons. First, I want to ensure the relevance of my points to the NLP community by describing a tool that would only be feasible to build given successful automatic detection and representation of historical events and their coreference relations. Second, a less ambitious vision would not as clearly demonstrate the gap separating historians' conceptualizations of events from those of analytic philosophers.

2 Individuating Events

The first requirement is *individuation.* To be able to individuate entities is to be able to distinguish them from others. Any system that consists of individual records describing entities presumes some way of individuating those entities. But in practice individuation is far from simple. Bibliographic organization, for example, is plagued by the problem of when to consider two documents to be "the same". The problem is worse for conceptual resources such as events. A semantic tool consisting of records identifying and describing events needs to employ some principles of individuation. The principles need to result in records with values sufficiently different that a user can distinguish between them and select the one he wants.

Philosophers have long debated how to individuate events. The problem is a deep one, as it is related to debates over the ontological status of events. To crudely simplify these debates, I characterize two basic positions, one which takes events to be concrete individual items in the world, and one which takes events to be products of language (specifically narrative language). My goal here is not to get into the specifics of the ontological debate but only to give a sense of the spectrum of different possible approaches to the individuation of events.

2.1 Events as Concrete Individual Things

The philosopher Donald Davidson believed that the structure of our natural language reflects the structure of reality. He argued that successful communication depends upon the communicators having "a largely correct, shared, view of the world" and that, since natural language is successfully used for communication, we can reach conclusions about the nature of the world by studying natural language (Davidson, 1977, p. 244). Using this approach to metaphysics, Davidson wrote a famous series of essays on the nature of events as indicated by our use of language (Davidson, 2001). The crux of his argument was that our use of language seems to indicate a difference between events and descriptions of events. Consider the following sentences:

1. Barack Obama signed the health care reform bill.
2. Barack Obama joyfully signed the health care reform bill with 22 pens in the East Room of the White House on March 23, 2010 (Stolberg and Pear, 2010).

Davidson argued that, intuitively, we want to say that these sentences all describe or refer to "the same event." If we trust our intuition we are led to believe that there is something in reality—the event—to which all these sentences refer. Davidson sought to bolster that intuition by demonstrating that, without the notion of an event as a concrete entity with a location in space and time, we cannot make sense of certain logical relationships among statements, for example the fact that each sentence in the list above is understood to entail the previous sentences.

Davidson argued that natural language sentences such as these can be translated into a "logical form" that captures their meanings and the relationships between their meanings. The logical form of a sentence is expressed using first-order logic. First-order logic is distinguished by its use of *quantifiers* to enable the expression of generalizations like *Everything that thinks is alive* (universal quantification) and assertions like *There is something that thinks* (existential quantification). Davidson held that sentences like the ones above existentially quantify over events. For example, the logical form of the second sentence above would be something like (paraphrasing first-order logic) *There exists something X such that it is the event of Barack Obama signing the health care reform bill, and X was done joyfully, and X was done with 22 pens*. What the logical forms of the sentences above have in common, Davidson believed, was this *X*, the event that is their shared referent and the existence of which they commonly assert, despite the different modifications that follow this assertion (Davidson, 2001a).

2.2 Events as Abstractions from Narratives

Davidson's argument, which I have not done justice to here, is a strong one and has become the mainstream position on events among analytic philosophers. Ideas like Davidson's lie behind efforts to automatically "detect" and "extract" events by analyzing texts. Certainly given sentences like the ones above, and the kinds of sentences Davidson typically uses as examples, the intuition that the sentences all "refer" to the same concrete event is strong. But consider the following sentences:

3. On March 23, 2010, with the strokes of 22 pens, Barack Obama transformed the United States into a socialist country.
4. On March 23, 2010, with the strokes of 22 pens, Barack Obama ensured a more equitable future for the children of the United States.

Do these sentences "refer" to "the same event" as the previous sentences? Let's assume that the context of these last two sentences is such that it is clear that the writer intended to comment upon the health care reform bill, and not something else Barack Obama did with a pen that day. On the one hand, it seems correct to say that these sentences too refer to the same event as the earlier sentences. But on the other hand, it doesn't seem incorrect to say that these sentences refer to two different events. The first event is one in which a closet radical who has managed to fool a capitalist country into electing him president finally realizes the first step in his secret agenda. The second event is one in which a liberal hero finally overcomes the forces of wealth and power to strike a blow for the little guy.

Sentences 3 and 4 are notable for their strong point of view. In that sense, they are more typical of the kind of sentences found in historical narratives. As the philosopher of history Frank Ankersmit (1983, p. 173) noted, "the differences between descriptions given by historians of what is still felt to be the same event may be of a more dramatic nature than in the case of scientific descriptions." As a result, the question of whether events can be separated from sentences becomes a little less clear. It becomes even less clear when one considers not just individual sentences, but whole texts. The historian William Cronon (1992) compared two books on the long drought that struck the Midwestern plains of the U.S. in the 1930s, known as the Dust Bowl. Cronon found that despite covering the same span of time and region of space, the two books constructed two very different Dust Bowls: one a triumph of human spirit over natural disaster, the other a human-wrought ecological disaster.

It was these kinds of contrasts that led the philosopher Louis Mink (1978) to claim that

> we cannot without confusion regard different narratives as differently emplotting the "same" events. We need a different way of thinking about narrative. "Events" (or more precisely, descriptions of events) are not the raw material out of which narratives are constructed; rather an event is an abstraction from a narrative. (p. 147)

Mink argued, contrary to Davidson, that events are not concrete things existing apart from and referred to by sentences, but are ways of summarizing sets of sentence organized into narratives. Of course, with his qualifying "more precisely, descriptions of events" Mink left the door open to the claim that he too was making a distinction between concrete events existing in the world and the sentences or parts of sentences describing those events. Mink's point, however, was that in history events and descriptions of events are interchangeable; we cannot identify events except by narrating them and deciding whether or not to conclude that two narratives are, in the abstract, sufficiently similar to say that they emplot the "same" events.

2.3 Criteria for Individuating Events

My view on the nature of events is closer to Mink's than it is to Davidson's. Yet Davidson is clearly right that there are times when we wish to say that two sentences refer to the same event, or that two texts have the same event as their subject. Without conclusively settling questions about the ontological status of events, we can nevertheless conclude that the criteria for individuating events can vary. We can see this by looking at how the two positions on the nature of events lead to different criteria for individuating them.

Davidson claimed that events are concrete individual things that we can count. He recognized that this claim, to be credible, required some principle for counting—some principle for deciding whether there is one event or two. In practice, Davidson (2001c) noted, we do seem to successfully count events, since "rings of the bell, major wars, eclipses of the moon and performances of *Lulu* can be counted as easily as pencils, pots and people" (p. 180). So, he asked, what are the criteria of individuation? He argued that

> Events are identical if and only if they have exactly the same causes and effects. Events have a unique position in the framework of causal relations between events in somewhat the way objects have a unique position in the spatial framework of objects. (Davidson, 2001c, p. 179)

Davidson's proposal is interesting because it

seems to suggest that Mink was correct when he argued that two narratives cannot differently emplot the "same" event. If to emplot an event is to place it in a nexus of causal and contingent relations, then two differently emplotted events are, under Davidson's criteria, two different events. But Davidson did not consider narratives to establish true causal relations. When Davidson wrote of the "causal nexus," he seemed to have in mind something like what Laplace's demon might see: the one true set of causal relations as determined by scientific laws. Historical narratives, on the other hand, he considered to be just "causal stories" or "rudimentary causal explanations" and not true causal relations, and thus presumably not suitable for individuating events (Davidson, 2001b, p. 161–162).

Later Davidson (1985), in response to a critique by Quine (1985), abandoned his proposal that causal relations individuate events. He accepted (with some reservations) the alternative criteria suggested by Quine that events are the same if they occupy the same space at the same time. This raises the problem of deciding deciding how, or whether, events occupy space and time. But both Quine and Davidson remained wedded to the idea that events are concrete individual things, and thus that there *are* some true set of individuation criteria for events, even though those criteria may be complex, and even though in many cases we may not be able to actually satisfy those criteria well enough to ascertain identity. In contrast, consider the historian Paul Veyne's (1984) declaration that

> events are not things, consistent objects, substances; they are a découpage we freely make in reality, an aggregate of the processes in which substances, men, and things interact. Events have no natural unity; one cannot ... cut them according to their true joints, because they have none. (p. 36–37)

Veyne argued that individuation criteria are not given by nature or language but are what we make of them. That is the position I take here. A semantic tool would need to propose some criteria for individuation, but there is no "true" set of criteria it must adhere to. Of course, the kinds of criteria suggested by Davidson and Quine are useful ones and the authors of a semantic tool might choose to use them, particularly if they wished to advocate a more "scientific" viewpoint. But these are not the only criteria, and authors might choose others or even more than one set of criteria. The main requirement is that authors document the choices they make.

An example of best practice for documenting individuation criteria was provided by Doerr et al. (2010) in the design of their time period thesaurus. Rather than assume that spatiotemporal location alone suffices to individuate periods, they made a distinction between the characteristics used to individuate time periods and the spatiotemporal regions associated with those periods. This made the thesaurus robust to new archaeological discoveries. For example, if a period were defined as being associated with the prevalence of a certain kind of pottery, then the later discovery that said pottery was in use earlier than was previously known would only result in a change to the temporal bounds associated with the period, not its individuation criteria.

3 Selecting Events and Documents

There are two main reasons why one might use a semantic tool to select event records. First, one may be interested in using the tool as a kind of reference resource, to acquire some basic knowledge of the event and its relations. Or one may wish to explicitly link a document to a particular event. For instance, a blogger who wishes to label a blog post as being about the Soweto Uprising might use a semantic tool to find a standard identifier for that event, which he can then use to link his post to the event record. In either case, the user would use some attribute or relation to select the event of interest.

3.1 Selecting Events

Most obviously, one can look for events by *name*. But most events do not have names, and in these cases, the event would need to be looked up via some entities or concepts to which it is related. There are a number of possibilities here. One might be interested in events involving some character, for example events in the life of Emma Goldman or events involving the Confederate States of America. Or one may be looking for events associated with or portrayed as occurring in a particular place or setting, such as Ireland or the American Midwest. Finally, one may look for events that are directly related to another event in some way that doesn't necessarily involve shared characters or settings. For example, one might seek events that have been portrayed as causes or consequences of the Battle of the Boyne, or all events that have been emplotted as leading up to, part of, or following from the French Revolution.

In addition to selecting events through their relationships to other concepts and entities, a semantic tool would support selecting events using the abstract grid of space and time. For example, one might be interested in events that took place within a given geographical area or that encompassed a given point on the globe. Similarly, one might look for events that took place during the 19th century or that were ongoing on June 4th, 2009. Finding events in space and time requires that events be resolvable to locations in a spatiotemporal reference system.

Finally, users might wish to select events of a certain type, such as battles or social movements. Given that one man's riot is another man's revolt, this can be more complicated than it first appears. To select events that have been typed a certain way, one would need to specify both a taxonomy of event types and possibly a party responsible for assigning types to events. Given the lack of standard event type taxonomies, it may be easier to rely on event name queries to approximate queries by type. Since named events often have types integrated into their names (e.g. the Watts *Riot* or the *Battle* of the Boyne), searches on event names may help select events of a certain type, especially if alternate names have been specified for events. For unnamed events, however, keyword searches on textual descriptions are unlikely to provide precise or complete results, and querying using an explicit type from a taxonomy would be preferable.

3.2 Selecting Documents Related to Events

But selecting an event may not be a user's goal but a means of finding an event-related document of some sort. A document can stand in two kinds of relation to an event. First, it may have been transformed into *evidence* for an event through the process of historical inquiry. In other words, some historian has studied the document, made a judgment about the status of the document as a survival from the past, and on the basis of that study and that judgment has inferred an event.

The historian Henri-Irénée Marrou (1966, pp. 133–137) enumerated a number of forms this inference from document-as-evidence to event can take. In some cases the inference may be very direct, as when the event in question involves the document itself, e.g. when it was produced, or when a certain word or phrase was first used. A slightly less direct form of inference moves from the document to some mental event, e.g. an intention, of the document's creator. Yet further afield are inferences made about the general milieu of the document's creator, inferences made on the basis of ideas expressed or the way they are expressed, regardless of the creator's specific intention. Finally there are those inferences made to events localized in time and space: things that characters in the past did or had happened to them. This last category of inferences is the least certain, despite the seemingly "concrete" or "factual" nature of the events inferred.

The second kind of relation that a document can bear to an event arises when the historian articulates his inferred event by producing a historical narrative. A historical monograph, historical documentary film, or a historical museum exhibit is a document that *portrays* an inferred event.

It is possible for a document to be both a portrayal of an event and evidence for some event. An eyewitness account is a portrait of an event, and if a historian has judged it to be authentic and accurate, it is also evidence for that event. Yet a document that is both portrait and evidence need not bear both relations to the same event. Marrou (1966, p. 135) gave the example of the work of fourth-century Roman historian Ammianus Marcellinus, which *portrays* events during the reigns of Constantius II and Julian the Apostate, yet which may be used as *evidence* for very different events, such as the appearance of particular ways of thinking or acting among a certain class of Roman men of that time, inferred from the language of the document.

When looking for documents related to an event, one may not be concerned with the kind of relation at all. In this case, if the event of interest is named, it may be sufficient to look for (variations of) the event name using full-text search of textual documents or of written descriptions of non-textual documents.

But this approach is unlikely to be either precise or comprehensive. Besides the well-known vocabulary problems that plague full-text search, there is the problem that documents which portray or evince an event may not use any names of that event. Expanding queries to include the names of people, places or other concepts related to the event may help, but to be reliably findable such documents would need to be explicitly linked to an identifier for the event.

Explicit linking to an event record would be indispensable if the *kind* of relation between the document and the event were important. One would need to be able to narrow down the set of all related documents to those that were related as evidence or those that are related as portraits, or to those that were related as both evidence and portrait. It might be desirable to further narrow the set by specifying *who* treated the documents as evidence or who created the portraits. The latter is a basic function of any bibliographic instrument. The former is rarely found in current tools, but will be increasingly important as the publishing of historical data becomes more widespread.

4 Contextualizing Events

While individuation and selection are necessary and useful functions, the effort of constructing a semantic tool for historical events would not be justified by these functions alone. Another key function of such a tool would be to provide *context* in an unfamiliar historical domain. As the historian Ann Rigney (1990) observed,

> There is a certain difficulty involved for a twentieth-century reader—particularly a reader who is not French—in following these nineteenth-century histories of the French Revolution (or indeed more recent ones) since they depend so largely on the reader's foreknowledge of a particular cultural code to which the principal elements of the Revolution already belong. (p. 40 n. 22)

A semantic tool could potentially help such a reader understand this code by linking events to time, place and related concepts, as well as putting them in the context of the narratives for which they act as mnemonics. To navigate this labyrinth of nested contexts, one needs a map:

> What information searchers need are maps that inform them about the world (and the literature about that world) in which they live and act. They need such maps in order to formulate questions in the first instance ... This is probably especially so in the humanities, where concepts are more clearly associated with worldviews. (Hjørland, 2007, p. 393)

A semantic tool for historical events would be a map informing users about the past and discourses about the past. Like a map of space, it could be used for both exploration and orientation.

4.1 Exploring the Past

A semantic tool for historical events would make it possible to learn about the past by following connections among events, characters and other concepts. The idea that the past is best understood through a network of contextual relations was dubbed "contextualism" by Hayden White (1973):

> The informing presupposition of Contextualism is that events can be explained by being set within the "context" of their occurrence. Why they occurred as they did is to be explained by the revelation of the specific relationships they bore to other events occurring in their circumambient historical space ... (p. 17)

A semantic tool for contextualizing historical events would thus be comparable to an outline of subjects for a history course, or a higher-level framework for organizing a series of syllabuses for history education. A syllabus or framework provides a map to help teachers and students find their way through a web of events and explanations. As students get older and become more capable, more detail can be added to the map. Any history is such a map in a certain sense. Ankersmit (1983) suggested that what makes historical narratives useful is that, like maps, they strip away the overwhelming detail of actual experience, leaving an intelligible form:

> A map should not be a copy of reality; if it were we could just as well look at reality itself. Being an abstraction of reality is just what makes maps so useful. The same goes for historiographies: we expect the historian to tell us only what was important in the past and not the "total past". (p. 51)

The intelligible form of a geographical map consists of the spatial relations made evident in its layout. One can look at a map to see where places are relative to other places. The map provides spatial context. A history provides historical context. One can read or watch history to learn how events happened relative to other events. The relations thus articulated in a history compose its intelligible form. Just as a simple hand-drawn route map can be easier to follow than a photorealistic one, a semantic tool would make these relations clearer through further abstraction.

The analogy with geographic maps raises the question of aggregation. Geographic maps of different regions can be transformed and projected onto a common system of coordinates. Can we expect to be able to merge semantic tools covering different domains of history to obtain a master tool covering a superset of these domains? According to Paul Ricœur (1984), we expect that

> the facts dealt with in historical works, when they are taken one at a time, interlock with one another in the manner of geographical maps, if the same rules of projection and scale are respected ... A secret dream of emulating the cartographer ... animates the historical enterprise. (p. 176)

Indeed, isn't the promise of being able to link together fragments of history into a collaborative whole one of the great motivations to develop standardized schematic representations of historical relationships? But we should not expect a single coherent past to emerge from such interlinking. We must remember that the relations in a semantic tool for historical events would be abstractions from historical narratives, which portray the past but are not the past itself. Different narratives express different points of view that do not necessarily combine into intelligible wholes.

Aggregating events into a larger framework would not yield a more complete view of the past, because there is no "whole view" of the past to be completed. However, a more complete view of *discourse about* the past could be achieved by juxtaposing different portraits made from different perspectives. To do this a semantic tool would need to accommodate conflicting views without trying to resolve them.

4.2 Orienting Oneself in Historical Discourse

A semantic tool that informed users about varying and possibly conflicting interpretations of past could be used for orientation. One may use a map to orient oneself by determining one's own position relative to something else. The philosopher Jörn Rüsen (2005, 1) has proposed that history is a "cultural framework of orientation" in time. According to Rüsen, we make the passage of time intelligible through reflecting on our experiences, interpreting and telling stories about them. Through such interpretation, the otherwise unintelligible passage of time acquires meaning and becomes history. History orients us in time: it tells us who we are and how we relate to what has come before.

According to Rüsen's theory, one way that people orient themselves using history is by tracing the kinds of threads White described in his account of contextualism. Genealogy, or seeking one's origins by tracing back through a web of births and marriages, is a good example of this. Other examples are stories told of the founding of an institution of which one is a member: the story of how Yahoo!'s founders started the company in a trailer at Stanford University is regularly recounted to new employees. These stories directly relate their audiences to historical characters and events, in effect making the audience members characters too.

But, as Rüsen showed, history does not perform its function of orientation only at this level of direct genealogical relations with the past. More often, history orients its audience at the level of interpretation, where histories are treated as stories rather than as transparently presenting inferred relations. For example, historians often allude to historical events as instructive examples for understanding current events. Consider the historian of early twenty-first century economic inequality in the U.S., who references the Gilded Age of the late nineteenth century. He does so not necessarily because he intends to trace causal relations between the earlier period and the later one. Rather he does so because he wishes to imply that the narrative that presents the best perspective for understanding the current situation is one that has a *form* similar to a particular, conventionally accepted narrative of the Gilded Age. He is making an analogy.

While analogies like the one above draw upon conventionally accepted narratives, other histories seek to re-orient their audiences by criticizing conventionally accepted narratives. To a certain extent, nearly every history attempts to do this—if the conventional story were perfectly adequate, why produce a new one? But certain histories specifically aim to dislodge a dominant narrative and replace it with a new one. Where analogies with the past appeal to a kind of continuity of form, critical histories try to break that continuity.

Finally, there are histories that try to orient their audiences not by directly linking them into historical narratives, nor by analogizing with or criticizing accepted historical narratives, but by giving accounts of changes in the narratives themselves. These histories re-establish continuity by portraying a higher-level process of change. An exemplary case is Thomas Kuhn's *The Structure of Scientific Revolutions* (1962), in which he posited that discontinuous change in scientific thought is itself a steady factor, something his late twentieth-century readers could use as a reference point for understanding their present situation.

What is important about Rüsen's typology of history is that it shows how history functions to orient us at the level of discourse and not simply at the level of direct chains of causal relation to the past. A semantic tool that was intended only to help people understand the past through exploration of the threads among events and characters and their settings would not need to refer to the stories that spun those threads. But if the tool were intended to help people orient themselves by understanding *discourse about* the past, it would need to represent not only events and characters and places but also the narratives that emplot them, and relations among these narratives.

Drawing upon Rüsen's ideas, Peter Lee (2004) developed a set of requirements for a framework for history education that would not only help students contextualize historical events but also develop their "metahistorical" understanding. Lee argued that students should understand not only what happened, but how we explain what happened. Lee argued that history education should simultaneously develop both students' conceptions of the past and their understanding of history as a discipline and discourse. These are the two functions that I have labeled "exploration" (of conceptions of the past) and "orientation" within historical discourse.

A semantic tool intended primarily to provide access to a homogeneous collection of documents, or to enable exploration of a narrowly defined slice of history, might simply summarize a single consensus story of the past. But a semantic tool for orienting users to a wider historical discourse would need to aid their understanding of the variety of stories told about the past, and to do so it would need to represent not only the contents of those stories—events, characters, settings—but the stories themselves.

5 Conclusion

The issues that I have raised here may seem far afield from the practical concerns of present day NLP research in medical informatics, topic detection and tracking, or natural language understanding. Certainly the development of a semantic tool for historical events is likely to be a much lower research priority than many other more immediate applications of automatic event detection and representation. But I have focused here on historical discourse simply because it puts the issues discussed into sharp focus, not because these issues are unique to the historical domain. No matter what the domain, NLP researchers working on systems for detecting and representing events will be forced to resolve the question of whether they are detecting and representing objectively existing things in the world or features of discourses about the world. And I believe that even the most "objective" areas of application that appear to need the former will eventually, like history, turn out to need the latter.

References

Frank R. Ankersmit. 1983. *Narrative Logic: A Semantic Analysis of the Historian's Language*. M. Nijhoff, The Hague.

William Cronon. 1992. A place for stories: Nature, history, and narrative. *The Journal of American History*, 78(4):1347–1376.

Donald Davidson. 1977. The method of truth in metaphysics. *Midwest Studies in Philosophy*, 2(1):244–254.

Donald Davidson. 1985. Reply to Quine on events. In E. LePore and B. P. McLaughlin (Eds.), *Actions and Events: Perspectives on the Philosophy of Donald Davidson* (pp. 172–176). Basil Blackwell, Oxford.

Donald Davidson. 2001. *Essays on Actions and Events* (2nd ed.). Clarendon Press, Oxford.

Donald Davidson. 2001a. The logical form of action sentences. In *Essays on Actions and Events* (2nd ed., pp. 105–122). Clarendon Press, Oxford.

Donald Davidson. 2001b. Causal relations. In *Essays on Actions and Events* (2nd ed., pp. 149–162). Clarendon Press, Oxford.

Donald Davidson. 2001c. The individuation of events. In *Essays on Actions and Events* (2nd ed., pp. 163–180). Clarendon Press, Oxford.

Martin Doerr, Athina Kritsotaki, and Steven Stead. 2010. Which period is it? A methodology to create thesauri of historical periods. In *Beyond the Artefact: Digital Interpretation of the Past*. Archaeolingua, Budapest.

Birger Hjørland. 2007. Semantics and knowledge organization. *Annual Review of Information Science and Technology*, 41:367–405.

Henri-Irénée Marrou. 1966. *The Meaning of History*. Helicon, Baltimore.

Thomas Kuhn. 1962. *The Structure of Scientific Revolutions*. University of Chicago Press, Chicago.

Peter Lee. 2004. "Walking backwards into tomorrow": Historical consciousness and understanding history. *International Journal of Historical Learning, Teaching and Research*, 4(1).

Louis O. Mink. 1978. Narrative form as a cognitive instrument. In R. H. Canary and H. Kozicki (Eds.), *The Writing of History: Literary Form and Historical Understanding* (pp. 129–149). University of Wisconsin Press, Madison, Wisconsin.

Willard Van Orman Quine. 1985. Events and reification. In E. LePore and B. P. McLaughlin (Eds.), *Actions and Events: Perspectives on the Philosophy of Donald Davidson* (pp. 162–171). Basil Blackwell, Oxford.

Paul Ricœur. 1984. *Time and Narrative*, volume 1. University of Chicago Press, Chicago.

Ann Rigney. 1990. *The Rhetoric of Historical Representation: Three Narrative Histories of the French Revolution*. Cambridge University Press, Cambridge.

Jörn Rüsen. 2005. *History: Narration, Interpretation, Orientation*. Berghahn Books, New York.

Sheryl Gay Stolberg and Robert Pear. 2010, March 23. Obama signs health care overhaul bill, with a flourish. *New York Times*.

Paul Veyne. 1984. *Writing History: Essay on Epistemology*. Wesleyan University Press, Middletown, Connecticut.

Hayden White. 1973. *Metahistory: The Historical Imagination in Nineteenth-Century Europe*. Johns Hopkins University Press, Baltimore.

Annotating Change of State for Clinical Events

Lucy Vanderwende
One Microsoft Way
Redmond, WA 98052
lucyv@microsoft.com

Fei Xia
University of Washington
Seattle, WA 98195
fxia@uw.edu

Meliha Yetisgen-Yildiz
University of Washington
Seattle, WA 98195
melihay@uw.edu

Abstract

Understanding the event structure of sentences and whole documents is an important step in being able to extract meaningful information from the text. Our task is the identification of phenotypes, specifically, pneumonia, from clinical narratives. In this paper, we consider the importance of identifying the change of state for events, in particular, events that measure and compare multiple states across time. Change of state is important to the clinical diagnosis of pneumonia; in the example "there are bibasilar opacities that are unchanged", the presence of *bibasilar opacities* alone may suggest pneumonia, but not when they are unchanged, which suggests the need to modify events with change of state information. Our corpus is comprised of chest X-ray reports, where we find many descriptions of change of state comparing the volume and density of the lungs and surrounding areas. We propose an annotation schema to capture this information as a tuple of <location, attribute, value, change-of-state, time-reference>.

1 Introduction

The narrative accompanying chest X-rays contains a wealth of information that is used to assess the health of a patient. X-rays are obviously a single snapshot in time, but the X-ray report narrative often makes either explicit or, more often, implicit reference to a previous X-ray. In this way, the sequence of X-ray reports is used not only to assess a patient's health at a moment in time but also to monitor change. Phenotypes such as pneumonia are consensus-defined diseases, which means that the diagnosis is typically established by human inspection of the data rather than by means of a test. Our recent efforts have focused on building a phenotype detection system. In order to train and evaluate the system, we asked medical experts to annotate the X-ray report with phenotype labels and to highlight the text snippets in the X-ray report that supported their phenotype labeling.

Analysis of the text snippets that support the labeling of pneumonia and the Clinical Pulmonary Infection Score (CPIS) reveal that most of these snippets mention a change of state or the lack of a change of state (i.e. persistent state). This is understandable given our task, which is to monitor patients for ventilator associated pneumonia (VAP), which can develop over time as a patient is kept on a ventilator for medical reasons.

Change of state (COS) is most often understood as an aspectual difference that is reflected in verb morphology (Comrie, 1976), where a state is described as initiating, continuing or terminating (see also Quirk et al., 1973, Section 3.36). In our corpus, however, COS is often reflected not in verbs, but more frequently in nouns. A careful analysis of our data indicates that the states expressed as nouns don't have the traditional aspects but rather exhibit COS more closely associated with comparatives, as they are susceptible to subjective and to objective measurement (Quirk et al., 1973, Section 5.38). These events compare two states across time or comparing one state against an accepted norm. Monitoring the state of the patient, and therefore comparing current state with previous states, is of paramount importance in the clinical scenario. We therefore propose in this paper to expand the annotation of COS to include the comparison of states over time.

2 The Task

Early detection and treatment of ventilator associated pneumonia (VAP) is important as it is the most common healthcare-associated infection in critically ill patients. Even short-term delays in appropriate antibiotic therapy for patients with VAP are associated with higher mortality rates, longer-term mechanical ventilation, and excessive hospital costs. Interpretation of meaningful information from the electronica medical records at the bedside is complicated by high data volume, lack of integrated data displays and text-based clinical reports that can only be reviewed by manual search. This cumbersome data management strategy obscures the subtle signs of early infection.

Our research goal is to build NLP systems that identify patients who are developing critical illnesses in a manner timely enough for early treatment. As a first step, we have built a system that determines whether a patient has pneumonia based on the patient's chest X-ray reports; see Figure 1 for an example.

01 CHEST, PORTABLE 1 VIEW
02 INDICATION:
03 Shortness of breath
04 COMPARISON: July 16 10 recent prior
05 FINDINGS:
06 Left central line, tip at mid-SVC.
07 Cardiac and mediastinal contours as before
08 No pneumothorax.
09 Lungs: Interval increase in right lung base
10 pulmonary opacity with air bronchograms,
11 increasing pneumonitis / atelectasis.

Figure 1. Sample chest X-ray report

2.1 Annotation

To train and evaluate the system, we created a corpus of 1344 chest X-ray reports from our institution (Xia and Yetisgen-Yildiz, 2012). Two annotators, one a general surgeon and the other a data analyst in a surgery department, read each report and determined whether the patient has pneumonia (PNA) and also what the clinical pulmonary infection score (CPIS) is for the patient. The CPIS is used to assist in the clinical diagnosis of VAP by predicting which patients will benefit from obtaining pulmonary cultures, an invasive procedure otherwise avoided. There are three possible labels for PNA: (2a) no suspicion (negative class), (2b) suspicion of PNA, and (2c) probable PNA (positive class). Likewise, there are three labels for CPIS: (1a) no infiltrate, report can include mention of edema or pleural effusion, (1b) diffuse infiltrate or atelectasis (i.e. reduced lung volume), and (1c) localized infiltrate, where one opacity is specifically highlighted and either PNA or infection is also mentioned.

In addition to the labels, we also asked the annotators to highlight the text snippet they used to assign the CPIS and PNA categories to reports (see (Yu et al., 2011) for similar approach to capturing expert knowledge). Thus, the snippets represent the support found for the CPIS and PNA label determination. The snippet found in lines 9-11, in figure 1, for example, was support for both the CPIS (1c) and the PNA label (2c).

2.2 Preliminary Results

We used this corpus to train two SVM classifiers, one for CPIS and the other for PNA, and evaluated them using 5-fold cross validation (for details, see Tepper et al., 2013). The micro F1-score of the CPIS classifier was 85.8% with unigram features and 85.2% with unigram+bigram features. The micro F1-score of the PNA classifier was 78.5% with unigrams and 78.0% with unigram+bigrams.

We analyzed errors made by the CPIS and PNA classifiers and observed that many of them were due to lack of in-depth semantic analysis of text. Consider the snippet "*The previously noted right upper lobe opacity consistent with right upper lobe collapse has resolved*", which is labeled in the gold standard 1A (no infiltrate). The system mislabeled it 1C, (localized infiltrate), because the snippet supports 1C entirely up until the crucial words "has resolved". This error analysis motivated the clinical event annotation task described in this paper.

3 Change of State for Clinical Events

In our data, clinically relevant events are often expressed as nouns. A text that mentions "a clear lung", for instance, implicitly describes the event of checking the lung density for that patient and finding it to be clear[1]. The TimeML annotation guidelines (Saurí et al., 2012) specify that states are to be annotated when they "identifiably change over the course of a document being marked up". In our scenario, where the document is the collection of the patient's medical notes during hospital stay, a noun phrase such as "lung capacity" is then a state that can certainly change over the course of the document.

Our corpus contains radiology reports and highlighted snippets of text where annotators found support for their finding. It is noteworthy that these snippets frequently describe observations of change, either in lung volume or in density. In fact, these changes of state (henceforth COS) appear more often in these snippets than non-snippets. Taking a random sample of 100 snippets, we found that 83/100 included some signal for COS, while a random sample of 100 non-snippet sentences included only 61/100 mentions of COS.

Let us consider some examples of snippets in which the clinical events, in italics, are referred to using nouns, a shorthand for examination / measurement of the noun in question. We have marked the signal words expressing a comparison across time in bold.

1. The *lungs* are clear.
2. *Lungs*: No focal opacities.
3. The *chest* is **otherwise unchanged**.
4. *Left base* opacity has **increased** and *right base* opacity **persists** which could represent atelectasis, aspiration, or pneumonia.

Snippets 1 and 2 describe states in the current X-ray report and do not express a COS. A close look at 3 and 4, however, reveals language that indicates that the experts are comparing the state in the current X-ray with at least one other X-ray for that patient and in doing so, are describing a COS. Consider the phrases "otherwise unchanged" in snippet 3, and "increased" and "persists" in snippet 4. Such words signal that the radiologist is examining more than one report at a time and making comparisons across these X-rays, without explicit reference to the other X-rays. There are other examples which exhibit explicit reference, for example, snippets 5 and 6, where the signal words and the explicit reference are in boldface, and the clinical events in italics:

5. *Bilateral lower lobe* opacities are **similar** to those seen on **DATE**
6. **Since the prior examination** *lung volumes* have **diminished**

Previous COS analyses (e.g., (Sun et al., 2013; Saurí, 2005)) have largely been limited to an analysis where events are expressed as verbs, and so is usually restricted to aspectual distinctions such as start, stop, and continue. In our data, however, many of the events are expressed as nouns and so we propose to extend the COS analysis to include measurements comparing two or more successive states and so will include concepts such as more, less, and equal[2].

4 Annotating change of state

While previous event annotation (Uzuner et al., 2010; Uzuner et al., 2011; Albright et al., 2013) marks multiple types of events, temporal expressions, and event relations, our annotation focuses on tracking changes in a patient's medical conditions. An event in our corpus is represented as a (loc, attr, val, cos, ref) tuple, where *loc* is the anatomical location (e.g., "lung"), *attr* is an attribute of the location that the event is about (e.g., "density"), *val* is a possible value for the attribute (e.g., "clear"), *cos* indicates the change of state for the attribute value compared to some previous report (e.g., "unchanged"), and *ref* is a link to the report(s) that the change of state is compared to (e.g., "prior examination"). Not all the fields in the tuple will be present in an event. When a field is absent, either it can be inferred from the context or it is unspecified.

[1] The guidelines for the 2012 i2b2 temporal relation challenge define events as "clinically relevant events and situations, symptoms, tests, procedures, ..." (Sun et al., 2013)

[2] In English, the morphology provides evidence, though rarely, that the comparative is a property of the change of state of an adjective. Consider the verb "redden", a derived form of the adjective "red", which means "to become more red", combining the inchoative and comparative (Chris Brockett, pc.)

The annotations for Snippets 1-6 are as follows: a dash indicates that the field is unspecified, and <...> indicates the field is unspecified but can be inferred from the location and the attribute value. For instance, the attribute value *clear* when referring to the location *lungs* implies that the attribute being discussed is the *density* of the lung.

Ex1: (lungs, <density>, clear, -, -)
Ex2: (lungs, <density>, no focal opacities, -, -)
Ex3: (chest, -, -, unchanged, -)
Ex4: (left base, <density>, opacity, increased, -), and (right base, <density>, opacity, persists, -)
Ex5: (Bilateral lower lobe, <density>, opacities, similar, DATE)
Ex6: (lung, volumes, -, diminished, prior examination)

A few points are worth noting. First, the mapping from the syntactic structure to fields in event tuples is many-to-many. For example, a noun phrase consisting of an adjective and noun may correspond to one or more fields in an event tuple. For instance, in the NP *left base opacity* in example 4, *left base* is *loc*, and *opacity* is *val*. In example 6, the NP *lung volumes* will be annotated with *lung* as loc and *volumes* as *attr*, but no *val*. Similarly, an adjective can be part of a *loc* (e.g., *bilateral* in example 5), a *val* (e.g., *clear* in example 1), or a *cos* (e.g., *unchanged* in example 3). Finally, the cos field may also be filled by a verb (e.g., *increase* and *persists*, in example 4). Making such distinctions will not be easy, especially for annotators with no medical training.

Second, events often have other attributes such as polarity (positive or negative) and modality (e.g., factual, conditional, possible). Most events in X-ray reports are positive and factual. We will add those attributes to our representations if needed.

5 Summary

Annotating events in a general domain without targeting a particular application can be challenging because it is often not clear what should be marked as an event. Our annotation focuses on the marking of COS in medical reports because COS is an important indicator of the patient's medical condition. We propose to extend COS analysis to include comparison of state over time.

We are currently annotating a corpus of X-ray reports with the COS events. Once the corpus is complete, we will use it to train a system to detect such events automatically. The events identified by the event detector will then be used as features for phenotype detection. We expect that the COS features will improve phenotype detection accuracy, in the same way that using features that encode negation and assertion types improves classification results as demonstrated by Bejan et al. (2012).

Our ultimate goal is to use event detection, phenotype detection, and other NLP systems to monitor patients' medical conditions over time and prompt physicians with early warning, and thus improve patient healthcare quality while reducing the overall cost of healthcare.

Acknowledgments

We wish to thank the anonymous reviewers for their comments and also our colleagues Heather Evans at UW Medicine, and Michael Tepper, Cosmin Bejan and Prescott Klassen at the University of Washington. This work is funded in part by Microsoft Research Connections and University of Washington Research Royalty Fund.

References

Daniel Albright, Arrick Lanfranchi, Anwen Fredriksen, William F. Styler IV, Colin Warner, Jena D. Hwang, Jinho D. Choi, Dmitry Dligach, Rodney D. Nielsen, James Martin, Wayne Ward, Martha Palmer, and Guergana K. Savova. 2013. *Towards comprehensive syntactic and semantic annotations of the clinical narrative*. Journal of American Medical Informatics Association (JAMIA). [Epub ahead of print].

Cosmin A. Bejan, Lucy Vanderwende, Fei Xia, and Meliha Yetisgen-Yildiz. 2013. *Assertion modeling and its role in clinical phenotype identification*. Journal of Biomedical Informatics, 46(1):68-74.

Bernard Comrie. 1976. *Aspect*. Cambridge Textbooks in Linguistics.

Randolph Quirk, Sidney Greenbaum, Geoffrey Leech, and Jan Svartvik, 1973. *A Grammar of Contemporary English*. . Longman Group Ltd, London

Roser Saurí, Jessica Littman, Bob Knippen, Robert Gaizauskas, Andrea Setzer, and James Pustejovsky. 2005. TimeML Annotation Guidelines Version 1.2.1. Manuscript, Available at http://www.timeml.org/site/publications/specs.html

Weiyi Sun, Anna Rumshisky, Ozlem Uzuner. 2013. Evaluating temporal relations in clinical text: 2012 i2b2 Challenge. In Journal of the American Medical

Informatics Association (JAMIA). Published Online First: 5 April 2013 10.1136/amiajnl-2013-001628.

Michael Tepper, Heather. Evans, Fei Xia, and Meliha Yetisgen-Yildiz. 2013. *Modeling Annotator Rationales with Application to Pneumonia Classification*. In Proceedings of Expanding the Boundaries of Health Informatics Using AI Workshop in conjunction with AAAI'2013.

Özlem Uzuner, Imre Solti, Fei Xia, and Eithon Cadag. 2010. *Community annotation experiment for ground truth generation for the i2b2 medication challenge*. Journal of American Medical Informatics Association (JAMIA), 17(5):519-23.

Özlem Uzuner, Brent R. South, Shuying Shen, and Scott L. DuVall. 2011. *2010 i2b2/VA challenge on concepts, assertions, and relations in clinical text*. Journal of American Medical Informatics Association (JAMIA), 18(5):552-556.

Fei Xia and Meliha Yetisgen-Yildiz. 2012. *Clinical corpus annotation: challenges and strategies*. In Proceedings of the Third Workshop on Building and Evaluating Resources for Biomedical Text Mining (BioTxtM'2012) in conjunction with the International Conference on Language Resources and Evaluation (LREC), Istanbul, Turkey.

Shipeng Yu, Faisal Farooq, Balaji Krishnapuram, and Bharat Rao. 2011. *Leveraging Rich Annotations to Improve Learning of Medical Concepts from Clinical Free Text*. In Proceedings of the ICML workshop on Learning from Unstructured Clinical Text. Bellevue, WA.

Author Index